Enou[gh]

'It took oodles of self-reflection before I came to realise my quirks developed into my resilience, my emotion gave me my empathy and my drama fuelled my passion. Too often I tried to fit in, when I was born to stand out.'

Throughout this book, Jana shares her life with you: the good, the bad and the ugly. Her stories of sport, medicine, divorce, loss, solo parenting – and media shenanigans – are told without embellishment or excuses. On her own admission: *'I often learned the hard way, battled against my will, rumbled with my demons, fought with self-acceptance, and boxed with negative inner chatter. I have always been too honest, shared too much and talked too fast.'*

But over the years, she's made peace with those demons, owning her flaws and choosing how to use her failures to become a stronger person – to the point where she now considers that the greatest success in life is believing in yourself.

Jana's life lessons are inspirational, not because of her achievements – stellar though they are – but because of her willingness to share with readers how to stare down your own doubts and fears and believe in yourself and your dreams.

This book is for anyone who has ever felt that they are not enough.

To my beautiful
rainbow family,
thanks for loving me
just the way I am. xx

enough

accept yourself, just the way you are

jana pittman

echo
PUBLISHING

'Jana is one of the most exceptional athletes Australia has ever produced. She reached the highest levels in one of the world's most competitive environments, athletics, before joining an elite handful of athletes to successfully become a dual Summer and Winter Olympian. Her commitment, passion and drive to succeed know no bounds, and following her stellar sporting career, she became a doctor while raising six children. Jana is not just an impressive sportsperson, she's an incredible human. It's been a real honour to follow her career and to work with her over the years. I hold her in the highest regard, and her incredible story is one that needs to be told.'

Mark Beretta OAM,
Sunrise and Seven Network sport presenter

'Jana's story is truly one of perseverance and determination. Despite facing many obstacles throughout her career, she has always been able to overcome them and come out on top. She is a role model for all aspiring athletes, doctors and mothers, and a shining example of what can be achieved with hard work and dedication. Jana has always been an incredibly driven, dedicated individual. She had two major career goals: an Olympic gold medal and a career in medicine. I witnessed her pursuit of Olympic glory; it was an uncompromising and inspiring journey. Tragically it was taken away from her days before her 400 m Athens Olympics race, when she was in world record shape. Jana transitioned the lessons she learnt on her Olympic journey into her future achievements in both her career and everyday life. Now she shares those lessons with others.'

Debbie Flintoff-King,
Olympic 400 m hurdles champion

'I truly know how inspirational Jana is. She's a fantastic role model to all generations and all genders.'

Mark 'Billy' Billingham,
SAS Australia

About the author

Two times world champion, four times Commonwealth champion – in the sport of athletics, Jana Pittman personifies resilience and determination. When continual injuries hampered her athletic career and could have signalled retirement, she swapped the track for the ice, joining the Australian women's bobsled team and becoming the first woman to represent Australia in both a Summer (2000, 2004) and Winter (2014) Olympic Games.

Off the track, Jana completed a Bachelor of Medicine, Bachelor of Surgery at Western Sydney University in 2019 (graduating with First Class Honours and the university medal), and is now a junior doctor in Women's Health. She completed a Masters of Reproductive Medicine at the University of New South Wales in 2020 and has initiated her PhD in Obstetrics (focusing on aspects of uterus transplantation).

This busy woman is proud mum to six children: Cornelis; little sisters Emily and Jemima; Charlie; and most recently, twins Quinlan and Willow.

Having experienced her own personal scare with cervical dysplasia, Jana became an ambassador for the Australian Cervical Cancer Foundation. In 2021, Jana was a participant in the gruelling television show *SAS Australia* on Channel 7. She made it to the last day of the course and was the final female standing among the 18 celebrity recruits, despite having given birth only five and a half months previously.

echo PUBLISHING

Echo Publishing
An imprint of Bonnier Books UK
4th Floor, Victoria House, Bloomsbury Square
London WC1B 4DA
www.echopublishing.com.au
www.bonnierbooks.co.uk

Copyright © Jana Pittman 2023

All rights reserved. Echo thanks you for buying an authorised edition of this book. In doing so, you are supporting writers and enabling Echo to publish more books and foster new talent. Thank you for complying with copyright laws by not reproducing or transmitting any part of this book by any means, electronic or mechanical – including storing in a retrieval system, photocopying, recording, scanning or distributing – without our prior written permission.

Echo Publishing acknowledges the traditional custodians of Country throughout Australia. We recognise their continuing connection to land, sea and waters. We pay our respects to Elders past and present.

First published 2023

Printed and bound in Australia by Griffin Press

MIX
Paper | Supporting responsible forestry
FSC® C018684

The paper this book is printed on is certified against the Forest Stewardship Council® Standards. Griffin Press holds chain of custody certification SCS-COC-001185. FSC® promotes environmentally responsible, socially beneficial and economically viable management of the world's forests.

Cover design: Lisa White

Back cover photo copyright © Jade Warne – Hipster Mum Photography

Page design and layout: transformer.com.au

A catalogue entry for this book is available from the National Library of Australia

ISBN: 9781760687991 (paperback)
ISBN: 9781760688004 (ebook)

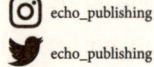

echo_publishing
echo_publishing
echopublishingaustralia

Contents

Foreword — 8

Organised chaos — 11
Courage — 17
Big dreamer — 25
Believe — 37
Heartache — 51
Failure — 69
The punches keep coming — 79
Phoenix rising — 95
A risk worth taking — 103
Enough — 115
Cut the fat — 135
Ownership — 147
My miracles — 163
A rainbow family — 179
Leaving it with you — 187

Thank you — 192

Foreword

Jana Pittman is a remarkable track athlete, doctor and mother of six. She is a two-time world champion in the 400 m hurdles and a multiple Commonwealth Games gold medallist. She has also represented Australia in the Olympic Games; however, Jana's achievements extend far beyond the track.

After suffering several injuries during her athletic career, Jana decided to pursue her other lifelong dream: to become a medical specialist. She graduated top of her class from the University of Western Sydney with a degree in medicine and is now a doctor. Jana's unique combination of athletic and medical expertise has made her an invaluable asset to the sports community. She has been a regular commentator on sports medicine and has also been involved in research on the effects of exercise on the body.

In addition to her athletic and medical achievements, Jana is a devoted mother to her six children. She has been open about the challenges of balancing her roles as an athlete, mother and doctor, but has always found a way to make it work. Jana is an inspiration to many, proving that with hard work, dedication and a positive attitude, it is possible to achieve great things in multiple areas of life.

I cannot quantify the admiration and inspiration I have developed for Jana across her life's journey. The words 'if', 'but', 'can't', 'never' and even 'maybe' are excluded from her thought processes.

I am indebted to her for the opportunity and privilege she provided as we committed to each other in the pursuit of climbing to the peak of world and Olympic glory.

Phil King, coach

Organised chaos

> Working towards success is like building a bonfire: every day you add a little more wood. One day all the preparation comes to fruition and you light the match - setting your dreams alight.
>
> **Jana Pittman**

It's a normal hectic school day, and we are already 10 minutes late for school kiss-and-drop. Cornelis, like a standard teen, is campaigning for canteen money because his lunch box is missing. Emily and Jemima are fighting over the bright purple hairbrush, their blonde locks still messily pulled back into yesterday's pigtails. My attention is squarely diverted to Charlie, my 18-month-old, who is busy escaping up the wooden staircase of our front living area. 'Charlie, buddy, wait for Mummy,' I holler. Too late ... I dart after him, my swollen pregnant belly swaying from side to side, arms stretched out to catch up. He turns, grins, and promptly loses balance, tripping over his little sneakers. I'd like to say I still have the lithe balance I once did as a world-class athlete, but this twin pregnancy has left me cumbersome and very clumsy. I catch the little rascal, but not before I too topple backwards, twisting in some fantastic somersault to land on all fours, my balloon belly millimetres off the wooden floorboards. It knocks the wind out of my sails. Wrangling my four kids out the front door is a success, but my stomach feels tight and unusually rigid.

After the kids are finally dropped off I drive across town, trying to avoid all the red lights and other school mums, thankfully arriving at my speaking gig with only 20 minutes to spare. Just enough time to collect my thoughts and have the obligatory pregnant pee. I love getting on stage and entertaining my audience. Especially today: I am 34 weeks and six days pregnant with my twins, my fifth and sixth children, living proof that with hard work, determination and a little bit of luck, you can have a wonderfully balanced life. On stage I share my story, flitting from Olympic sport, to medicine, to motherhood; the dreams, the failures, the pleasures and heartaches. I am, and always will be, an open book.

Today, every few minutes, my stomach churns and my womb tightens. During my 45 minute presentation,

I count four, maybe five, unusual tightenings. I finish off the explosion of questions after my presentation and take a few pictures with those wanting a keepsake. The waves in my womb continue; mild, but enough to punctuate my thoughts. Extracting myself from the crowd, I decide to pop in to the hospital for a quick check-up, especially after the fall this morning. Of course, I drive myself there ... idiot.

Although my body isn't ready, these babies have other plans. What I thought had been mild cramping is the start of my fifth labour. Over the following hours we battle through the ups and downs of the birth; my body takes over as I try to breathe (and growl) through my contractions. At 11 pm my gorgeous little boy Quinlan enters the world, all arms and legs. Then, in perfect parallel with the rest of my life, my second twin, little Willow, decides she's not keen on this evacuation order and flips into a dangerous transverse position. She is stuck. Bas Gerges, my obstetrician, prepared for this possibility, reaches in and attempts to grab her little feet, with no luck. She's not ready to budge. He moves over and examines Quinlan, who's already camped on my chest, taking a breather like it's no big deal.

As a junior doctor I know that if we can't get Willow out I will need a caesarean section, or there is a chance that something worse could happen. *Whatever it takes, just be safe my little one.* I casually keep one eye on the clock as six, eight, 10 minutes pass; the other eye is on Bas, amazed at how calm he remains. 'Are you ready?' He goes in a second time.

Holding my breath, I watch his facial expression for any giveaways that he has been successful. Then in a matter of seconds, I see these tiny toes squeezed between his fingers, followed by a pair of legs and the cutest little wrinkly bum I have ever seen. She was making a spectacular entrance, coming out feet first; what we call in obstetrics a breech extraction. I push gently to deliver her head and soon both Willow and Quinlan are lying together in my arms. Breathless, I look down at the utter perfection in these two tiny cherub faces. I am now a mum of six.

> **I am proud of the life I have lived and can't wait to see where the next chapter takes me.**

When I was trying to decide which memory to commence this book with – something from sport, motherhood, or my career as a doctor – it had several beginnings until I settled on this one, the story of what will likely be my last birth. The day of my twin labour reflects my life perfectly. It was rushed but simple, busy but planned, the kids were the centre of my day and there was enough excitement to keep me on my toes. It was organised chaos.

In this book I will share my life with you: the good, the bad and the ugly. Through anecdotes about sport, medicine, divorce, loss, solo parenting and media shenanigans, my life will unfold for your viewing. I am proud of the life I have lived and can't wait to see where the next chapter takes me; however, it wasn't always like that. I often learned the hard way, battled against my will, rumbled with my demons, fought with self-acceptance and boxed with negative inner chatter. I have always been too honest, shared too much and talked too fast. It took oodles of self-reflection before I realised that my quirks developed into my resilience, my emotion gave me my empathy and my drama fuelled my passion. Too often I tried to fit in when I was born to stand out.

Each chapter of this book is a step in my journey; a life lesson I have learned, often the hard way. I hope it inspires you to conquer your own dreams and rethink your own value. I hope you read it and find peace, but also a new zest for goals that might be lying dormant. People often ask me what my next big life dream is; I have a few crazy ideas, but my number one goal is to help someone else see how beautiful they are, just the way they are.

Each chapter starts with a quote. I love hearing from inspiring people and think we can learn so much from others who have already paved the way before us. Each quote has been gifted to me by its author and I now pass their wisdom on to you.

Courage

> If you think you can, or if you think you can't, you are probably right.
>
> **Debbie Flintoff-King**
> *(Olympic 400 m hurdles champion)*

She screamed as she hit the water, her stomach taking the brunt of her fall. Sitting perched on a nearby boulder, I watched each of the remaining *SAS Australia* recruits take on the crazy cliff dive. We were each given a chance to fall backwards off a 10 metre rocky outcrop with the aim of landing headfirst in the icy water. Most recruits crumpled at the waist, flipped over or fell sideways. One jumped off, the idea of a spinal injury too much for her to push through the fear.

Directing Staff (DS) Foxy called my number: 'Right, Number Four, you're up. Go-go-go.' Startled, I jumped up and ran off across the rugged bush track, leaving the remaining few who were yet to dive huddled together in anticipation. I could see DS Billy gesturing for me to run towards him. I slowed down, welcoming the chance to catch my breath, my adrenalin sky high, my heart racing. In his thick British accent Billy said, 'Number Four, just follow instructions, it's not rocket science, this task is about listening.' I scrambled further up the hill to where DS Ant Middleton was waiting to scare me off the edge. He gestured for me to walk out onto a wooden plank, secured to the precarious cliff face, and peer over the edge to the water below. Vertigo threatened to end my challenge before I even had a crack! 'Don't tilt your head back, keep your body straight, hold on with your abs; don't overthink this Number Four, just let your body fall and it will slice through the air like a knife and cleanly enter the water. If you don't listen, you get hurt.' These were Ant's parting words of wisdom.

The DS called me a 'lioness' on the show, but all that really means is I had courage to keep going when things got tough.

I crept out onto the edge, my heart pounding, my legs shaking. It would have been so easy to hand in my number: the way to exit this celebrity challenge and go home to my kids and the security of my sofa. Then the familiar little voice that always joins me when I step out of my comfort zone thankfully surfaced: *Come on, Jana, life is always a choice – you don't have to do this. I can give you permission to quit, but then your failure is guaranteed. Or you can try – give it a crack – and then failure is only a chance.* I closed my eyes and fell.

Everyone is afraid. I can't lie: I appear to hide my fear well, but it bubbles up regularly and keeps me in check. In 2021 when I signed up to do Channel 7's *SAS Australia* – a gruelling celebrity TV program where a bunch of well-known Aussies challenge themselves in a special forces–style selection course – I was petrified on many levels. Worried I would look a fool, scared I would say the wrong thing, and afraid my aging ex-athlete body, which had carried a baby only a few months before, wouldn't be up to the challenge. I signed up for several reasons: firstly, my brother Ryan had served in the Australian Army, doing a tour in Afghanistan, and I wanted to get a tiny peek at what he had experienced in his training; secondly, I loved the idea of doing a truly tough course and testing my inner reserve. It didn't let me down: they gassed us, they drowned us, they shoved us in ice baths and threw us out of helicopters. It was amazing!

Lastly, after having my fourth baby, I really needed a training goal. Yes, I need a goal to push myself physically. I may have been an 'animal' in my athletic days, but now I was a mum of many and a tired junior doctor, so I had plenty of excuses to roll over in bed for five more minutes sleep. Doing this TV show gave me some accountability, forced me to challenge myself and get back out of my comfort zone.

I also learned to love that feeling of fear, the adrenalin rush it brings, the shiver down my spine. The DS called me a 'lioness' on the show, but all that really means is I had courage to keep going when things got tough.

It helps that I have a little 'warrior' voice that kicks in when things get difficult, drawing that lioness out, coaxing me to remember the first time I gave in to fear and the consequences that followed. Let me take you back to the day when a poor decision taught me a great deal about the power of our inner voices, both positive and negative.

Brush with fame

I was 16 years old. I was so excited, as a budding teen athlete, to receive the call-up from Athletics Australia to race against some of Australia's greatest track athletes: Lee Naylor, Tamsyn Lewis and Cathy Freeman. This was the first time I would line up against these 'big guns' and I was beyond ecstatic. I hadn't broken 54 seconds over 400 metres at this point, so these ladies were due to beat me by more than 20 metres.

We all started warming up; I was jittery with excitement. I followed them around, jogging a little too close to Cathy for her comfort, stretching side by side with Tamsyn and doing sprints with her, too. I was enamoured with my heroes. Into the call room we went, had our names and numbers marked off and took our seats. At this point, as athletes do, several of us filed off to the bathroom for a last-minute nervous pee. And this is where it all seemed to change. I was sitting there in my cubicle when overwhelming fear consumed my mind: a horrible little voice chanting to me that I didn't deserve to be there, that I would look like a fool, that they were so much better than me, harping on that I would be demolished. Suddenly, my hamstring felt very sore, so sore I couldn't bend over to adjust my shoelaces. I limped to the basin to wash my hands; nope, no improvement – it was still tight. Hobbling back to the call room, I handed in my lane number and withdrew from the race. I shuffled off to a grassy hill to watch the race, my race, the chance of a lifetime to run against these incredible women and I was sidelined with injury ... or was I?

Did I really have a sore hamstring, or could I have pushed through it? The gun went off and as I watched in silence a much worse pain ripped through me: the pain of failing myself; the pain of letting fear get in the way of opportunity; the realisation that I had just sabotaged myself. I had given into my own insecurities. There was nothing wrong with my hamstring, it was an excuse. From that day on and for weeks to come, I wrote the same saying in my sports journal: 'You can try and fail, or fail for simply not even trying.'

That memory of letting *myself* get in the way of my goals is one that I always carry with me. Eventually I learned to overcome my doubts, but it didn't happen overnight: for a long time there was a battle of will, fear versus courage competing in my mind. But I kept working on it and every race thereafter I used as an opportunity to hone my ability to push past my doubts. With time and practice my inner lioness grew, and now it dominates, coming out just when I need to be told to take a chill pill and give the challenge a crack. Don't get me wrong: my little saboteur voice still tries to weigh in, but I am now better at telling her to bugger off.

Fear simply means that the thing you are trying to do holds meaning for you; it shows you are passionate about the challenge. So do not walk away from the thing your fear response shows you that you love! Accept your fear and reframe it: yes, you can try to achieve your goal and *fail*, but there is also a chance you might be *successful*. Pushing through your fear is an opportunity to prove to yourself how brave you are. The more you get out of your comfort zone and walk the uneasy path of fear, the quicker your courage grows.

LIFE LESSONS

Life is a constant series of choices, and failure is only one of the possible results. Success is also an option.

* You can try, and fail; or you can fail by simply not trying.

* Don't let your doubts and fears get in the way of reaching for your goals.

* Fear teaches you what is important to you. Let your inner beast loose.

Big dreamer

> **Seek your passion; love what you do and you will never work a day in your life.**
>
> **Phil King**
> *(Coach to both Debbie Flintoff-King and me)*

Waking, you instantly know it's the day; you feel like you have waited a lifetime for this moment to arrive. The 2003 World Championships final. Your stomach churns like you are riding a giant roller-coaster. Your heart rate accelerates, pumping so hard it overwhelms all your other senses. People say it's like butterflies – *yeah, right*: this is like giant tiger claws digging away at your insides.

Today is judgement day. Have you pushed hard enough; is there a stone left unturned? Reality continues to hit you in perfectly timed waves, a shiver runs up and down your spine and you recognise it as utter fear coursing through your veins. Yet you know the foundations are laid and your inner beast is ready to roar. Today is the day to set the track alight.

Sadly, it's only morning, and you know the day will drag on. Tick-tock, tick-tock, the clock yawns through the hours in apparent slow motion. You fluff around, barely eat, struggle to breathe – and the nerves remain all consuming!

Finally 4 pm arrives and, from that moment on, life revs into sixth gear. Before you know it, you're entering the stadium to start your warm-up and plugging in your headphones: *Rocky III*'s 'Eye of the Tiger' your motivational companion for the evening. Your coach stands a few feet away gently feeding you words of encouragement, reminding you of the hours of sweat and tears that were poured into your program. Then the stadium radio bursts into life: 'Could the participants in the 400 m hurdles final please make your way to the call room.' Boom: those tiger claws return in full force.

You collect your things, check your bib number and slip into the call room. It's just a small demountable set up for the games, but somehow it feels daunting. Eight empty white seats, no pictures, and a toilet at one end. The other athletes file in, have their names and numbers marked off and take their seats. Everyone is fidgeting, knees bouncing, eyeing each other off. Most act like they own the place: jumping up, yelling out and running on the spot. Others hide in the corner. You just watch.

You don't have to wait long before you are escorted to the next holding station, your spikes and bags are checked, your lane number is allocated. Then you're ushered out into the enormous stadium: a hundred thousand people screaming their lungs out, ringing cowbells and banging on the advertising posts. The gun goes for the race before yours and you struggle to hold down the titbits of food you'd managed to swallow hours before. Your whole body quivers with anticipation.

Everyone is fidgeting, knees bouncing, eyeing each other off. Most act like they own the place: jumping up, yelling out and running on the spot. Others hide in the corner. You just watch.

The officials lead you past the finish line. The stadium lights are so bright, it's very apparent you are in the spotlight as you make your way to the starting blocks. The crowd already ripples with excited energy, and you hear your name chanted several times.

Finally, the starter calls you to your mark, you strip off your green-and-gold Aussie tracksuit and readjust your shoelaces. You take a deep, slow breath and picture yourself flying around the 400 m track, clearing the 10 hurdles like a cheetah after its prey. Suddenly all the nerves of the day, the stress and the pressure float away into the crowd, leaving you bulletproof and ready. The champion emerges, the mind is ready: the competition arena is your playground.

'On your marks' ... *Oh wow, here we go. Breathe ...* 'Set' ... *Please, please execute ...* Bang! It's now or never. The beast is free.

You explode out of the blocks and attack the first hurdle; gliding over it, you dig deep and attack the next. The speed in your legs comes easily as you fly down the back straight.

> **Don't give up now. Ignore the heaviness in your legs, pick up your knees, pump your arms! Battle with the fear, fight off the pain, release your mind ... let your body do the work.**

The world record holder from Russia is in the lane outside you, moving so fast. By the 200 metre mark she is already eight metres in front. The American is going stride for stride and the Polish girl is breathing down your neck. *Hold onto your reins, forward with the chest, flow the bend ... the others will come back to you. Patience.* You all approach the final turn and it happens: the world feels like it's in slow motion. The American stumbles and it's just you, hot on the heels of the Russian. As you stalk your opponent you notice their stride is shortening, their power fading: their tank is empty. Changing gears, you set out for the kill. With every metre your target draws closer. With only 50 metres to go and one final barrier left to conquer, you glide over that last hurdle and dig so deep your lungs are on fire.

The finish line approaches swiftly and you edge out in front. The other athletes are panting hard around you. *Come on, keep pushing. Don't give up now. Ignore the heaviness in your legs, pick up your knees, pump your arms! Battle with the fear, fight off the pain, release your mind ... let your body do the work.* The noise in the stadium erupts as you finally blast through the finish line. *First* ... you have done it! *First* ... you heard it, the new world champion! On this day you make history for Australia.

A good attitude

I grew up in a family where my brother and I were encouraged to dream big and set wildly fabulous goals. So, while most parents might have gently laughed when their eight-year-old daughter declared she wanted to be an Olympian, my dad started racing me up the hills of our little hobby farm on the outskirts of Sydney, trying to avoid the piles of horse poo that littered the grass.

Dad is my hero and my mother is my greatest ally. Growing up, we lived comfortably because my father worked his butt off 360 days of the year; the other five were when he came to support me at the athletics track and cheer from the sidelines. I still remember it like it was yesterday. As you already know, I was always a jangle of nerves, my stomach in knots and the fear a constant companion. Dad would warm me up and try to shake off the doubt. Just before I would go into the call room, where they marshall you before a race, he would pull me aside and give me a few words of encouragement. 'Now, Jana, how fast are you?' 'As fast as a cheetah,' I would reply. 'How strong are you?' Dad questioned. 'As strong as five lions,' I would answer. 'What are we here to do?' he would chant back. 'We are here to win.' My final words as I headed off into the tent.

I know how intense this sounds, but Dad never applied pressure when it came to the outcome; success was not measured by the place I finished but by the effort I put in. He just wanted me to have a shot at accomplishing my dreams. Dad was the one who taught me the relationship between success and hard work; that a good attitude is one of the only things you can directly control.

Setting goals

At the same tender age that I dreamed of becoming an Olympian, my aspirations to become a doctor evolved. I regularly dressed up in kiddie scrubs and subjected my poor brother to fake operations and administrations of several unusual concoctions I had mixed up. We were quite lucky he didn't end up in hospital as a result of my overactive imagination! So, while racing for our country on the international stage was a dream come true, the day I graduated from medical school takes top spot on my career podium. It took two decades longer to come to fruition, but it was worth every sacrifice.

> **Often these days when I do motivational speaking gigs, I ask the audience to take a minute, collect their thoughts and rank their goals in order of which 'dream' they aspire to achieve most.**

My third childhood dream became a reality the year I wrote this book. As a youngster I already knew I wanted to be a mother and used to announce to anyone who would listen that I planned to have five children. This was usually received with a 'good for you' or 'it takes two to tango'. Little did they know I would end up as a mum of six, including having my middle two daughters as a solo parent via anonymous sperm donation.

Both these goals have their own chapters, but they have a place here under my dreams. These days, when I do motivational speaking gigs, I often ask the audience to take a minute, collect their thoughts and rank their goals in order of which 'dream' they aspire to achieve most.

Interestingly, many can't do this. Maybe they aren't aware of what they want to tackle, they have too many ideas, or they have someone else's goals at the centre of their life; for example, a partner or child's goals.

While I think it is incredibly admirable to put your own goals aside, and be the plus-one to someone else's success, having something that is just yours is important, for several reasons: life changes, relationships break up, kids move out and then you have to shift gears and find a new you.

Sitting down and thinking about something (or lots of things) that you would find fulfilling, is worthwhile. When I was a kid I had a dream board: I would cut scraps from magazines and pin them up alongside signed autographs from my heroes. It had a countdown to the next big race and my school timetable with exam dates. It was the inner workings of my brain spewed out onto a giant whiteboard. Every few months I would show my coach or parents and ask them to add quotes, update programs or include other ideas to help me make my dreams come true. Why was this important? Because first you need to discover what your dreams are. Then, by writing them down, or in my case pinning them up, you step out of the 'contemplating' phase and into the 'planning' stages.

Sharing your goals with others ensures that you have accountability. There is nothing worse than when you announce to a colleague, 'I am going to write a book' and when you run into them six months later and they ask, 'How's your book going?' you have to give excuses as to why it never got off the ground. But even if this does happen and you haven't made inroads into your goal – after all, we are all human and have lives to live – then the question from them can be a great reminder to kick your dream back into gear.

When I was a kid I had a dream board: I would cut scraps from magazines and pin them up alongside signed autographs from my heroes.

So dream big and bold. Establish what it is you really want to achieve in your life, write it down and share it with a few key people who can help keep it alive and kicking. For me it was sport, becoming a doctor and having lots of kids. Along the way I have added to my dream board, which is now in the form of a diary.

My dreams evolved to include finding a second Olympic sport (bobsled), opening a sports business (failed miserably) and joining the cast of *SAS Australia* (just awesome), to name a few things. My diary is full of scribbles and mind maps, as my passions grow in different directions. Of course, there are short-term goals, such as losing weight after my recent pregnancy or conquering a marathon, and long-term goals such as finishing the doctorate I have just started and my speciality training in medicine.

Some of these dreams will come to fruition, while others will founder and perhaps be replaced by even more interesting ideas. I am a big believer that when one goal fails, you should have a hard look at it (for me that requires a good cry) and then replace it straight away with another idea you have had on the backburner. In a later chapter, I'll talk more about how to deal with the crushing blows of failure (of which I have had many).

Long-term success depends on how you view those setbacks: they can defeat you and break your confidence or be the flame that ignites your next dream.

LIFE LESSONS

Whether you dreamed of being an astronaut or an artist when you grew up, hang on to these ambitions and use them to motivate and challenge yourself. Even as they continue to evolve, your childhood dreams, as well as your adult aspirations, should remain the driving forces in your life.

* You need to learn to push through your fear and pain to strive for your goals.

* Hard work may not always lead to success, but it builds confidence.

* There are lots of things you can't control, but you *can* control your attitude.

* Keep your dreams alive by allowing them to evolve with the changes in your life.

Believe

> **A champion attitude always brings about champion results. Where there is great effort there are great performances.**
>
> **Jacqui Cooper**
> *(World champion and Olympian in aerial skiing)*

I have always loved to run. The speed in my legs comes easily to me, and I love the wind in my hair, the freedom of moving my body, arms pumping, breathing heavily, heart racing. It's in my blood. Mum always says I never crawled or walked, but stood up and sprinted down the hallway. I was a natural.

When I was a child, as good as I was at running, I was equally bad at social interactions. I felt alive and confident while doing sport, I had a wonderful loving family at home, but school was altogether a different experience. Remember the tall, awkward girl? Well, that was me. The strange one who befriended the teachers and was just a little weird? Yep, that was me too. I was the ultimate nerd: I had my hair cut short like a boy, I spoke too fast and I did a little too well in my exams.

My parents consistently praised excellence and taught me to be proud of my achievements, but this was not something my peers always appreciated. In fact, other kids found me intimidating right from the start. Sadly, I desperately wanted to be liked, but never knew the right words to say to the other kids, which left me often bullied and – even more often – alone at lunchtime. When I was running, however, I was already a lioness: fast and lean, my body perfect for this endeavour.

Kids at the track might have found me scary, too, but they had similar quirks to me, so therefore we bonded over sports drinks and protein bars. Running was my escape. I loved to compete and, from the age of 10, running became a weekly event.

Competitions were a chance to test my speed; however, within a few years, my raw talent proved to be inadequate and I started losing races to athletes who had trained. My parents didn't believe in structured training for me at such a young age; they thought school was far more important. In the early years, I joined forces with several wonderful local Little Athletics coaches – Mrs Mac, Mr Charles Tees and Mr Wayne Clarke – under whom my love for sprinting and hurdling evolved.

In truth, I don't think my family realised I had a future in sport until the day Jackie Byrnes, who was the coach for Melinda Gainsford Taylor (she was one of my childhood heroes), asked me to join their squad and be Mel's training partner ahead of the Sydney 2000 Olympics.

> **Seek out a hero and copy and learn from them, using them as proof that dreams can become reality.**

School social activities continued to be a disaster zone, while my track life started to blossom. I sought solace in every hard training session and pleasure in the weekend races. I really blossomed under Jackie's guidance. Her squad was full of top junior and senior athletes. Naturally, I just copied everything Melinda did. (I still do this now, as an adult: seek out a hero and copy and learn from them, using them as proof that dreams can become reality.)

Mel was a marvel. I used to watch her lift massive weights with ease, and her running was effortless. When I was a kid, she dominated me on the track: although I was already taller than her, she was so powerful and fast. We would practise starts together and, even with a decent head start, I was often left in her wake. She was also one of the kindest and most gentle souls; and it can't have been easy for her, having a constant chatterbox like me as her shadow.

Another girl, Astrid Loch-Wilkinson, was also in the same training squad. She would later become my bobsled pilot for the 2014 Winter Olympic Games in Sochi, Russia.

Changing track

I continued running throughout my teenage years, battling competing school commitments and an ever-increasing track program. Our training progressed at a rapid rate and my times dropped in huge chunks. Jackie had asked another coach, Ukrainian Fira Dvoskina, to step in and improve my hurdling. I mention this, because it is rare in sport for coaches to recognise when they need to employ the expertise of others. It was such a strength of Jackie to work so fluidly with Fira, who had a great technical eye for hurdling.

In mid-1999, I won my first World Youth title in the 400 m hurdles in Bydgoszcz, Poland. This was the first time I heard our beautiful Australian national anthem boom through the stadium as they hung that gold medal around my neck. It was breathtaking, and I vividly remember thinking my goal to make the Athens 2004 Olympics was burgeoning.

I went back to Australia and trained really hard over the summer, doubling up my physical loading, pushing my weights and ploughing through the grass-running sessions. The following year was going to be tough, as

I faced the World Junior Championships in Chile as well as my final year of high school. While I was happily distracted by sport, I still wanted to qualify for an undergraduate degree worthy of later getting me a place studying medicine.

Knuckling down, I studied in my school lunch breaks and with a torch in the car on the way home from training, my poor mother not even able to listen to the radio as I pored over my biology notes. Crazy early mornings, cross-training in the swimming pool, then racing to catch the bus so as not to be late for roll call. I was commonly squeezing in a quick run on the school oval or bolting up some stairs in the quadrangle in my free periods. It was nuts!

Olympic dreams

My dream of making the Olympics was well fuelled, as every day there was news about the coming Sydney Olympic Games: 'One year to go till the opening ceremony', 'Who will light the Olympic cauldron?', 'Stadium Australia ready to roar'. I was beyond excited at the chance to watch Cathy Freeman compete in my hometown, minutes from my school.

As the games rapidly approached, like most young athletes I applied to carry a 'basket' during the big events. At such championships, the athletes strip off their gear at the start line and place their belongings in one of the plastic baskets lined up behind their blocks. In complete synchronisation, their belongings are picked up by 'basket carriers' and marched off the track to await the athlete in the post-race media zone. I was over the moon when the letter arrived announcing I would be one such basket carrier. I would be within touching distance of some of the greatest athletes in the world.

Then the stadium speaker burst into life, informing me and the crowd that I had just run an Olympic qualification time for the 4 x 400 m relay!

It was about nine months before the Sydney Olympic Games. Although I was now often competing in the open women's events, I still contested the Australian All Schools Championships. Due to the copious amount of studying I was doing in preparation for my New South Wales Higher School Certificate, my expectations were fairly low. Mel GT and I had clocked some great times in training, but there is a huge difference between training and the competition arena.

They were using the Olympic warm-up track as the venue for the championships and I loved the idea of racing on a track that would soon host the world's greatest athletes. I love my imagery, so on the day I pretended to be an Olympian: I slipped on my headphones and set off for my usual two-lap jog, stretch and run throughs, before floating over a few hurdles and checking myself into the call room, visualising all the way through that it was the Olympic Games.

I won the 400 m hurdles in a decent time, but made a few technical errors that we could easily massage out with time. Then the final of the 400 m track race (not the hurdles) rolled around. It was a gusty, hot summer day, typical of Sydney in December. I knew I had to go very hard out from the blocks and into the back straight as there was what we call a 'headwind', meaning the wind fought back at you and hit you in the face. I did just that: 'balls to the wall', we used to say – leave nothing in the tank.

I thought I had gone too hard: there was still 100 metres to go and I could already feel the burden of fatigue like a massive weight on my back, the lactic acid pulling down my legs, but my stride didn't shorten. All that speed work with Mel GT paid off as, before I knew it, I was storming across the finish line and searching for the clock to check my time.

My lungs were on fire, I was bent over trying to fight off the dizziness, when suddenly I heard this rip-roaring 'WAHOOOOOO' sounding through the stadium. Jackie's voice was unmistakable. Suddenly she was hurdling the side rail and running onto the track screaming, 'You little beauty!' and pointing at the clock.

I could see the huge fluorescent yellow numbers flashing my new personal best time of 51.81 seconds, but then the stadium speaker burst into life, informing me and the crowd that I had just run an Olympic qualification time for the 4 x 400 m relay! For athletes to make the Olympic Games there are set performance times you must run to be considered for selection. Somehow, I had done the impossible. Forget Athens, I was going to the Sydney 2000 Olympic Games!

Believing in myself

My first Olympics in Sydney was amazing. I didn't make it out of the heats in my individual 400 m hurdles event, but I helped the Aussie women's 4 x 400 m team make the final. The crowd was beyond extraordinary: running at an Olympic Games is like being at a nightclub on steroids; the level of noise is deafening. I had always had the belief, had visualised the outcomes and surrounded myself with the right people. Belief goes a long way if you just let yourself dream and throw fear to the wind.

After this monumental first Olympics I was lucky – well, perhaps more than just lucky, I was privileged – to compete for my country almost weekly for over a decade. In the same year as the Olympics, I won double gold at the World Junior Championships while simultaneously sitting my New South Wales Higher School Certificate exams in the Australian Embassy in Chile at 2 am!

After this, my senior or open women's career took off. In the chapter called Courage, near the start of this book, I talked about my greatest race: winning my first senior world title in Paris, France, in 2003. In track and field, the Olympics and the World Championships are our most coveted events. If you are Australian, you prefer to win the Olympics, as it's more prestigious, but many American athletes report a preference to win the World Championships: you get paid more for it, and more athletes can run.

> *I had always had the belief, had visualised the outcomes and surrounded myself with the right people. Belief goes a long way if you just let yourself dream and throw fear to the wind.*

This is because the Olympics is about country participation with a maximum of three athletes allowed per country per event; whereas at the World Championships, the reigning world champion is given a chance to defend their title, so theoretically there could be four Americans in the final!

Statistically speaking, in my event the Americans often have the season's six to eight best athletes. In other words, if it was just about being the best in the world, the

Americans could hand out world titles and minor medals at their national championships.

The day I won my first world title, I knocked off the current world record holder from Russia and a swag of other superstar 400 m hurdlers. I vividly remember crossing the finish line: my body felt like it didn't belong to me, my mind swirled around, eyes drinking in the stadium, heady with adrenalin.

After you win a title like this, you head off on a victory lap to acknowledge the die-hard fans. The crowd goes wild as you jog past, stopping occasionally for a photo or signature. Then you enter the media zone, where the camera flashes blind your eyes to which journalist is firing excited questions at you. It's all so surreal. Then they escort you to the obligatory drug test, which takes hours, because you are so dehydrated.

> *I found my village: my family, my coaches and my friends who all believed in me as well and helped me to keep following my dreams.*

Four years after my first win, in 2007 I won the same event in Osaka, Japan. This second world title was even more unexpected, as I had given birth to my son Cornelis only eight months prior to the race. I had lost many of my sponsors when I announced I was pregnant, because they didn't believe in me. But *we* believed it was possible and, if there was ever a time I was happy to be right, it was then.

Making memories

Coupled with these world titles were a few other wonderful highlights, such as double gold at the Manchester Commonwealth Games in the 400 m hurdles and 4 x 400 m relay, and again double gold in the same two events at the Melbourne Commonwealth Games in 2006. I had moved to Victoria by this time, and was training with Phil King, the husband and coach of superstar hurdler Debbie Flintoff-King, who had herself brought home Olympic gold from the 1988 Seoul Olympic Games.

The Melbourne Commonwealth Games was as close as I got to feeling what Cathy Freeman must have felt at the Sydney Olympics: winning in front of a home crowd and soaking up the atmosphere of booming Aussie fans as I did the victory lap. It was definitely my most memorable medal ceremony too, when the Australian flag rose higher than all the other nations' flags and the vast majority of the audience sang 'Australians all, let us rejoice' at the top of their lungs.

Throughout these years of competing and success on the track, the thing that kept me going was belief in myself and my dreams. Despite the bullies, the critics and the sponsors who lost faith in me, I came through with flying colours. I found my village: my family, my coaches and my friends who all believed in me as well and helped me to keep following my dreams. Whatever your dreams are, surround yourself with those who will help you to believe in yourself – and to find your inner strength and ability.

LIFE LESSONS

Accepting who you are and believing in yourself can be the key to finding success and making your big dreams come true.

* Find your strengths, explore them, question them and then use them to build dreams for your future.

* Remind yourself that heartbreak is just another lesson in resilience: once you live through it, you prove that you are capable of surviving it.

* There are times when life commitments (such as doing my final high school exams and running in the Olympics and World Junior Championships) could have been a distraction, but I was able to push past the doubt and find the motivation.

* When your dreams become reality, roll with it! You've proved yourself right.

Heartache

> **Being resilient is understanding you won't always win. You will likely lose more than you win. So it is important to celebrate the wins when they happen, for they are indeed rare, and acknowledge the battle, the fight, the adversity that's been overcome in order to achieve it.**
>
> **Anna Meares**
> *(Multiple Olympic and world cycling champion)*

Well, this is going to be a big chapter ...

Before we get started, I want to acknowledge and honour that many of my failures and tough times are relatively trivial compared to what has gone on in the world over the past few years. I've seen a lot, having worked as a doctor on the front line through COVID-19;

being scared half to death when my dad stayed in his little country town as fires were ripping through only a kilometre away; and hearing the despair as people lost everything in floods. My heart goes out to all of you.

The way we deal with heartache and failure changes throughout our lives: some of us come out more resilient and stronger, while others struggle to recover. The following chapters reflect my opinion on heartache and recovery: they are just ponderings from someone who is often called 'resilient', although in truth I am only human, with several defence mechanisms and coping strategies that possibly have helped along the way. I want to share those with you: they may not resonate, but I hope they get you thinking and chatting with your loved ones about what puts you back on track.

Breakdown

There were three weeks to go before my second Olympic Games in Athens, 2004. In Sydney 2000, my first Olympics, I had been more a spectator than a contestant. Things were very different now: I was the reigning world champion, the reigning Commonwealth champion and hadn't been beaten internationally for the whole season. My coach was Phil King. Phil is an incredible coach; tough and driven, but he would have given me the shirt off his back. Despite owning several swim centres, he coached me full time, charging me nothing, simply content with the race victories we collected together. Just incredible really.

The final race prior to the Games was the prestigious Weltklasse Zurich, then a Golden League event. I was so nervous, I was buzzing with fear. We got to the warm-up area nice and early. The Stadion Letzigrund is different from most international stadiums; it doesn't have an independent warm-up track, just a strip of Tartan (all-weather track) about 150 metres long, underneath the stands. The Australian media had turned up in droves to capture our last race.

In truth I am only human, with several defence mechanisms and coping strategies that possibly have helped along the way.

My body felt incredible. Only a week earlier I had broken the world record in a training run here in Zurich. I was on fire, and I couldn't wait to explode onto the track and strongly mark my territory for the coming Olympic Games.

Gliding through my warm-up, the usual *Rocky* music thrummed in my ears, the beat setting the rhythm for my strides. Only 15 minutes to go till the call room. A couple more drills and we were ready.

Phil set up the six hurdles a few metres apart for me to do a specific hip-opening drill called the 'running spider'. I would run and vault over them, swapping one leg over for the next. Usually, the hurdles are two metres apart, but I was feeling so good I asked Phil to stretch them apart a little further; after all, if you want to smash records, you need to push the envelope.

The first few were awesome. I felt like a gazelle flying across the track. One more to go and then it happened. The pain was excruciating, but the sound that snapped through the air as the meniscus in my right knee tore in half still haunts me. My physiotherapist standing just five metres away heard the bang, sending him running towards me, just in time to catch my collapsing weight. I tried to hobble along and go for a jog, resurrect my warm-up, but I could barely place weight on the leg. I dropped onto my hands and knees. Something had broken and it broke me too.

We were rushed to the first-aid room and soon I was in an ambulance on my way to the local hospital for the imaging that would determine my fate. The media had gone berserk, taking copious photos of my tear-stained face. The MRI results confirmed I was badly injured. I had torn my lateral meniscus in an awkward way that would require surgery if I was ever to run again.

We saw the best Swiss surgeon, who had operated on many of the greatest athletes. He confirmed that my Olympic campaign was over and told me that he feared for the rest of my running career. He booked me in for surgery and I went back to the hotel in utter shock. Less than three hours ago I was on target to make history; now I was a blubbering mess. It is an athlete's worst nightmare. I sat there and wolfed my way through about a kilogram of chocolate. What did it matter anyway? My Olympic dream was over.

Hope

Back home, the media was in a frenzy about my downfall. The stories took off like wildfire. Prior to this, I had only ever had positive media, stories of success and triumph. This was the start of the 'Jana Saga' in which I would end up overpublicised and very much hurt by some of the dramatic headlines that would follow. Initially, however, it helped.

A surgeon in England, Fares Haddad, had seen the world's press about my injury and called the Australian team doctor, saying, 'Please come and see me for a second opinion. Don't give up hope yet.' Phil and I jumped at the chance, always ones for pushing boundaries and defying the odds.

Before I knew it, we were on a plane to London – and then camped in the consultation room. 'I won't know till I get in there, but there is a chance I can fix this well enough for you to run in two weeks.' *What? Run at the Olympics?* This was unbelievable. *One surgeon says I may never run again, and this guy thinks he can save my Olympics. Impossible!*

We had nothing to lose. The deal was, he would open up my knee and make the decision under the knife. If he could simply cut the broken cartilage away, we would be on; if it required stapling and a reconstruction, my games were over. I put my Olympics and the rest of my running career in his hands.

> *I ran races in my head so as not to lose the rhythm and tried to picture myself standing on the podium, victorious, in Athens.*

The very next day I was lying on the operating table, drifting off to sleep, a million thoughts running through my head. Dr Haddad had let our Aussie team doctor, Tim Barbour, and Phil come into the theatre to watch the operation. It was a comfort having them by my side. Lights out.

I woke sleepily to Phil holding my hand and smiling like all our Christmases had come at once. 'Well?' I asked, and he replied, 'JP, they did it! You should have seen the angles they put your leg in. It is stable. We can do this. We can still win!'

Within a few hours, I was up and hobbling around. There was very little pain, just grogginess.

From that point on, the Olympic Gold campaign was reignited. We had two weeks until the games. Debbie Flintoff-King had flown over from Australia. Having trained as a naturopath after her Olympic brilliance, she took up the challenge of getting me to the start line in Athens in the best shape possible. It was pretty special, having one of your Olympic heroes in your own pit crew! Debbie went scouring the local villages looking for homeopathic remedies to help speed up my recovery. I would lie down and visualise the tissue repairing, imagining it healing and knitting together.

I couldn't run for the first week, but I ran races in my head so as not to lose the rhythm and tried to picture myself standing on the podium, victorious, in Athens. My Australian medical team were incredible: Andrew Lambart (my personal physiotherapist), combined with Brent Kirkbride (the team physio) and Tim Barbour, worked tirelessly to get my body back in one piece. Hours of slow stability work, massages and acupuncture.

Back on track

It was time. We were ready to go. We packed our things and returned to the airport en route to Athens. I felt oddly calm: maybe it was all the meditating or maybe I had moved past the fear into the unknown. We had no control now. What would be, would be.

Once in the Olympic village I did my first tentative track session, a few run throughs, and some stretching. We had five days till the start of competition – the surgery was now more than a week ago, but I hadn't run for 10 days. It was daunting, and every muscle rippled under the stress and fear of another pop or spasm.

My mind was full of 'what ifs' and challenges. I watched the other athletes, especially some of the girls in my event, gliding over hurdles or doing electric starts out from the blocks. They looked free and ready. Was I?

The Olympics are always a place of intense emotion, and time ground to a halt. There was little to do but eat, sleep, stretch, and wait out the time. Those five days felt like an eternity. I did have one fabulous afternoon when Peter Brock and Laurie Lawrence came to take me for coffee. I am sure Phil organised it. It was customary to bring in a superstar athlete from the past to inspire and motivate the team. My dad had been a massive car-racing fan, so I had grown up watching Brocky conquer the Bathurst raceway. Now here he was, telling me not to dwell on my injury and to make the most of this awesome opportunity. Combine this with Laurie, who was a renowned coach and motivator, informing me that Grant Hackett had won gold in the Olympic 1500 m swimming final with half a lung, so I could win mine on one leg. They filled my room with a haze of positivity – and they also adorned my bedside table with a giant boxing kangaroo to keep me in the right frame of mind.

Finally, the day of competition rolled around. In my event there is a heat, semifinal and final. Each round would lay dreams by the wayside and whittle down the field to only eight athletes, the world's best. The previous two times I had competed at this level my whole focus had been on winning, my mind fixated on the time I ran and whether I could lower my personal best. Today, during the heats, I was numb and quiet. I hadn't been over a hurdle since the injury, so it was going to be a rather interesting morning. In truth, I felt I had run out of feelings; or perhaps I was holding them deep down inside me. It was surreal. The warm-up went smoothly, and I felt quite normal. It was remarkable. My legs felt strong and fresh. Maybe there was going to be a fairytale ending after all.

I glided over the hurdles. My touch-down times weren't brilliant, but they would get me through. I repeatedly chanted to myself: *One race at a time, Jana. Be patient.*

Then the loudspeakers boomed out our race call. It was time. I gave Phil a big hug and wandered off down the tunnel towards the call room. In Athens it was a long distance from the warm-up track to the main stadium. Like death row, you walked out to your fate. They hold you for an agonising 45 minutes as they check and recheck your things. It's a lot of time to eye off the other competitors, lose your nerve or grow your spirit.

Finally, we were escorted out past the roaring crowd and onto the magnificent track. The hurdles were there waiting for us, in their perfectly pristine rows. I had painted an Aussie flag on my bad knee with the words 'Dare to Dream' written on it. A reminder to me, and anyone who could see it, that the impossible is possible. We are so much stronger than we think we are. I had defied the odds, and here I was about to run at the Olympic Games, merely two weeks after massive knee surgery. I felt my chest puff out.

> **I had painted an Aussie flag on my bad knee with the words 'Dare to Dream' written on it. A reminder to me, and anyone who could see it, that the impossible is possible.**

I had done this many, many times. This wasn't the unknown, this was home. Breathing in the atmosphere, I set up my blocks for the heats. If I could make it past the first round, if my knee held up, we were in with a shot.

The gun fired and off we went. My rhythm was wayward, but it didn't matter – the hurdles came flying up at me anyway. Through the first 200 metres I was comfortably in front, and entering the home straight I maintained my lead. Oh my goodness, it felt so good. I was back and firing. How was this possible? Crossing the line first, I felt triumphant and on top of the world. The press went crazy with excitement. I spoke briefly to the hordes before swiftly returning to the warm-up track to cool down and prepare for tomorrow: the semifinal.

Wrapped in Phil's arms, I celebrated. If nothing else, we had made it. Whatever happened now was just a bonus. The semifinal went almost identically to the heats. I did feel a little fatigue in my legs, which was natural since I hadn't run for two weeks. I raced Yuliya Pechonkina, my Russian nemesis and still the world record holder. She edged in front of me in an electric time of 53.31 seconds. The most alarming of all was the Greek girl I had faced and beaten only a few weeks before in Heraklion, Fani Halkia. She was running out of her skin, clocking a massive PB, dropping a full second off her personal best and setting a new Olympic record in 52.77 seconds in the second semifinal. The track was fast!

Before I knew it, I was on the bus, on my way to the track for the final. Phil was sitting quietly next to me. The buzz between us was palpable. There was nothing more we could do. Fate would play out today. At the track I warmed up quietly. I didn't feel like music this time. My thoughts were so busy already, the music would only heighten my arousal. Over the last warm-up hurdle, I felt the first slight buckle in my knee. A tiny loss of power and a chance for my mind to spin into overdrive: *Push on, Pittman, you will be fine. You can't change it now.* I didn't tell Phil, there was no point worrying him unnecessarily.

Soon, for the final time, I was walking down the long concrete corridor towards the track and my destiny. Eight women, all Olympic finalists, waiting to fight it out. I can't remember walking into the stadium – the pressure was so consuming. In fact, I can't remember much of the race itself. I don't remember being called to my blocks or my name being announced, and the usual buzz of the crowd has also been lost. I don't remember the starter's gun going off, I can't recall the sound of the girls panting around me. I have no memory of the usual floating feeling down the back straight or making any attack through the bend.

Just as it was then, it is still all a blank: until the moment I reached the eighth hurdle, with 100 metres to go, and my knee buckled under the weight of my body. It was only a momentary incident, but it brought me back to reality. Suddenly, I was acutely aware of everything around me. Fani Halkia was a few metres ahead, Yuliya Pechonkina was right beside me, with a few other girls also in the thick of it. I tried to push and gain those lost few metres, to recapture the power, but for the first time in my entire life my will had gone, my tank was empty. As they pulled further away, I tensed and lost more ground, spiralling into a world of frustration. I was losing! My mind reeled from the intense feeling of being out of control, unable to fight back, unable to increase the speed of my slowing legs. With one hurdle to go, the medals were clearly out of my reach. It may only have been split seconds, but it felt like an eternity for me, as I slowed down crossing the line. It was over. I had lost, not even medalled.

Heartbreak and beyond

After the race I was in shock, with all the emotion of the last few weeks weighing heavily on my shoulders. I watched as Fani Halkia grabbed the Greek flag and ran triumphantly around the track on her victory lap. That had been me, this time last year at the World Championships. I was escorted to the media bay to face my fate. I spoke briefly, congratulating the winners and keeping face, all the while desperate to remove myself to the quiet of the warm-up track. Back to Phil and Debbie.

Finally, after I escaped from prying eyes, I let the tears run. They started slowly, just a trickle that would go unnoticed, but by the time I had reached the warm-down arena they were torrential. All the pain and stress of the past few weeks, not to mention the past year, the sacrifices and loss we had worked through, came rip-roaring out.

Phil was there waiting for me. I flew into his arms, which only induced more tears. We were heartbroken. The 2004 Athens Olympic fairytale had ended.

Elusive success

Fast-forward two years to Melbourne, 2006, and there I was preparing for my second Commonwealth Games. I was now being coached by Chris Rawlinson, a former 400 m hurdler from England, also the reigning Commonwealth champion, and who soon after these games would become my husband. After Athens, Phil King and I had parted ways, much to my regret now. The reasons we both concluded were around the pain and intensity of the Athens loss, but in truth I should have fought harder and found solutions to the issues we faced, as we had unfinished business.

These games were being held in what was then my hometown, just as the Sydney Olympics had been. What a buzz! The athletes' village was a short bus ride from the centre of Melbourne, and they used many of the same venues as the 1956 Olympics, which also meant we would be running inside the Melbourne Cricket Ground, home to some of Australia's greatest sporting moments.

Our preparation for the meet was yet again hampered by injuries, but we made it to the race day in enough shape to be in with a chance to defend my Commonwealth title from Manchester.

I breezed through the heats and soon it was time for the final. Our names and lane numbers were confirmed, and the competitors were whisked out into the massive arena. We stripped off and waited nervously behind our blocks for the announcer to call our race to attention and the starter to set us off. The stadium was bursting with excitement and anticipation. It was literally overflowing. A home-crowd victory was calling me.

Slowly, the stadium radio announced the finalists' names, as one by one we were called out and honoured by the crowd. I am usually so laser-focused. I simply gave an obligatory salute, but tried hard to keep my game face on, completely in the zone. As they announced my name this time, along with the fact I was the reigning Commonwealth champion here to defend my title, the crowd literally went wild. Many people even got up out of their seats to cheer. It momentarily but beautifully broke my attention. I looked around the 80,000-seat stadium and sucked in the support and excitement. All the Aussie flags waving madly overwhelmed my senses. I felt such joy at their response I could barely hold back my emotions. It gave me the biggest pre-race boost imaginable.

> *I am indebted to the wonderful Aussie spirit that pumped through me. Crossing the line victorious in front of a home crowd is truly a gift.*

The gun went off and I felt like I was running on the crowd's enthusiasm. I could even hear them cheering down the back straight. Over the last hurdle it was impossibly loud and, while my legs were burning with fatigue and lactic acid, the Australian public carried me home. I am indebted to the wonderful Aussie spirit that pumped through me. Crossing the line victorious in front of a home crowd is truly a gift.

The medal ceremony was one of the highlights of my life, standing there on top of the podium singing our anthem at the top of my lungs alongside the majority of the crowd. It made all the sacrifices and sadness from losing Athens pale into insignificance. I was back!

LIFE LESSONS

Heartache is inevitable in life, but there are strategies you can use to make yourself more resilient when it hits you.

* Heartache can strike suddenly and be devastating, but you can look for hope.

* Assemble a team of friends and family who will support you no matter what.

* Draw on that great Aussie spirit that runs through all of our veins and never give up hope.

Failure

> There is no owner's manual in life, we learn through our actions and experiences. Don't beat yourself up about the mistakes you have made, be aware of them, own them, learn from them, and grow. They can be a blessing.
>
> **Mark Philippoussis**
> *(Two Davis Cup titles, twice Wimbledon finalist, former world tennis star)*

Things continued to go from strength to strength athletically when, a year later, in 2007, I brought home a gold medal from the World Championships in Osaka, Japan, just eight months after the birth of Cornelis. I was now double world and double Commonwealth champion; my times were electric, and the world record was creeping closer and closer with every brutal training session I pumped out. This was the perfect preparation, with only 12 months until the Beijing Olympic Games. Bring it on!

Early in the next Olympic year, I was on fire. My times continued to leave me in awe of my training program and my team and I were giddy with excitement.

One particular day we were at Homebush in Sydney, where I was training with an Irish athlete. We planned to do about a dozen race-pace efforts over 60 metres. I gave her a small head start so we would hit the line together. We set off, legs pumping, muscles rippling. I was chasing her down inch by inch. Just as I pulled up level and tried to stretch out and improve my margin, I heard a familiar huge snap, and pain seared through my toe, scorching its way up into my right foot. I'd had a niggle in this toe since the Osaka World Championships victory a few months prior, but had ignored it, determined not to miss a day of training and spoil my chance of Olympic glory.

As usual we went straight in for an MRI, which unfortunately revealed the toe needed to be operated on – and the whole Athens debacle exploded back into my mind. *Are you kidding me? Is this for real? Surely this can't be happening again.* The one thing that we had in our favour is that this time we still had several months to regroup. I was incredibly lucky that one of Australia's top orthopaedic surgeons, Dr Mark Blackney, who specialises in feet and ankles, agreed to squeeze me into his already busy schedule. I jumped on a plane and flew down to Melbourne to see him. My husband stayed home with our little son Cornelis, so I went alone.

The actual surgery went brilliantly. Dr Blackney managed to operate on my tiny second toe joint arthroscopically, which meant a tiny incision and minimal recovery time. I was literally walking a few days later and running on a treadmill within the week. I had long wanted to be a doctor, but events like this further fuelled my interest in the field.

A fortnight later we flew to Beijing for a photo shoot for Adidas, my major sponsor. All their international athletes had to go; however, it was the middle of winter, and the snow was falling heavily. We drove to the 'Bird's Nest', which would soon be the stadium and home for the XXIX Olympic Games. There they stripped us off to our tiny race kits in minus 10 degrees Celsius weather, posing us for photos on a crazily tall podium just outside the stadium, depicting an Olympic victory that was surely to come.

> **I haven't raced many Aussie seasons at all, with the constant barrage of injuries my silly old body has been faced with.**

Inspired by our trip, we arrived home and jumped straight into running fast. Too quickly, as it turned out. I was compensating for the toe injury and shifting my weight through the other leg, often hobbling like a wounded wildebeest. Soon this compensation had me also carrying a very sore Achilles tendon. Once again, this forced me to miss the Australian domestic season, including the 2008 Olympic selection trials. I haven't raced many Aussie seasons at all, with the constant barrage of injuries my silly old body has been faced with. Nevertheless, my win at the World Championships in 2007 had given me automatic selection to Beijing. So my team and I fought on.

Disappointment

Around the end of March 2008, it became clear that my body just wasn't up to the training. My left plantar fascia was problematic, and I had a host of other niggles. It was like someone had a voodoo doll in my image and was pricking it all over. I was starting to feel rather desperate. I had been told about an incredible doctor in Germany called Dr Hans-Wilhelm Müller-Wohlfahrt. A number of top international athletes had consulted him when their bodies were broken. The clock was ticking, and I was going from bad to worse, so Chris and I flew over to try and resurrect this third Olympic campaign.

The therapy was certainly interesting. I thought Australia was a leader in sports medicine, but this was a step above anything I had seen. Dr Müller-Wohlfahrt's clinic had its own MRI and scanning machines on site, not something we had in Australia. In the four days we were in Munich, I had over 150 injections; some were small and pain free, others made my skin crawl. The injections were the latest legal therapies. I also had thick, tar-like stuff put on my Achilles. It stank to high heaven and I still have no idea what it was for. I certainly felt like a giant smelly pincushion. I didn't care ... whatever it took, within the legal limits of sport.

> **One session I was on fire, the next I could barely walk. This roller-coaster of training and injuries continued once we got to Europe, desperately trying to hold onto a glimmer of hope.**

A few weeks later I was back, running well, but the roller-coaster continued. Just as we landed in the United States for a training camp, my Achilles reared its ugly head again. One session I was on fire, the next I could barely walk. This roller-coaster of training and injuries continued once we got to Europe, desperately trying to hold onto a glimmer of hope. My support team tried everything: stretching, ice, massage, chiropractor, but nothing settled it.

My heart was breaking into little pieces as I watched yet another Olympics slipping through my fingers.

Athens had almost been easier; it happened right before the Games, and it was a freak accident. This one was months out, so my dream had to die a slow, ugly death.

With six weeks to go till the 2008 Olympics, I broke down from utter exhaustion. I had another injury in Loughborough, UK, where we were based, and the MRI report revealed yet another torn plantar fascia – the third in my career. We just couldn't catch a break. This never-ending turmoil took a toll on my marriage, too. Chris and I fought that night, debating whether I should pull out of the Games. I can't begin to describe how this felt. Even writing this I can feel the knot sitting at the back of my throat. Another Olympics down the drain.

But we couldn't stop now; we still had a few weeks, and I knew I had the ability to recover quickly. The only choice I had now was to inject my foot with local anaesthetic before each training session and strap it – it felt like a robotic foot, it was held so immobile. We got through another week of training like this and my times, while nothing special, were improving.

The final hurdle came just a month before the opening ceremony. My body was strapped to the max and I was running a flat-out, race-pace 150 metre repetition with the boys in the team. I set out fast, attacked the bend and opened in the straight. Twenty metres before the line – *pop* – my calf muscle on the opposite leg tore.

I was done.

History repeats

It's hard to believe, but the very same thing happened four years later at the 2012 London Olympic Games. We were training the house down and a few months prior to the games I partially tore my plantar fascia again. If it had torn completely, the pain would have been bearable, but it was hanging on by a thread of tissue, leaving me crippled. Desperate to make the Olympics, I remembered a story about Robert Harvey, an AFL footballer, jumping off a box and ripping off the rest of his plantar fascia, allowing him to play on. So, I decided to give this a crack.

I ran repeatedly over 60 metres, the pain searing through my foot, but it didn't feel like it had released entirely. I then swapped to jumping down off the steps. I continued to run and jump until I was dehydrated from the tears. I have never felt pain like this in my life. It was worse than childbirth. Surely it had worked.

Sadly, an MRI the next day revealed it remained only a partial tear, the one time in my career when I wanted a full rupture. How ironic.

Another Olympic dream was shattered, making it three games in a row. Three dreams ripped up and lost to devastating injuries. I am aware that it is just sport, but at the time nothing could fill the emptiness that seeped into my bones. The constant questioning that filled my every waking moment was unbearable. It was everything I had ever known, everything I had fought for. Why was I being punished? How could I win so many international championships, but not the only one that mattered to me? The hours of training, the weekly vomiting as my body was pushed beyond its limits, the operations, the countless injections, and the sacrifices my whole team had made – all washed away with my dreams, yet again. I felt like an utter failure. The flame was out.

What comes next?

When failure strikes, you can use the setback to fuel another dream. Explore the pain, feel the hurt, let it out and then grab the reins and drive yourself towards a new goal. Reignite an old idea or create a new plan to conquer a failure; flip it on its head. Instead of running from an opportunity because you are afraid of a repeated flop, use the fact you survived the anguish to extinguish any fear that comes with a new opportunity.

After all, if we don't succeed at the next goal, the worst that can happen is that we'll be left feeling just like we do right now. So, the only way is up! When the doubt creeps in, simply say, 'No thank you, Negativity. I am a survivor, and I am angry that fate didn't allow me to achieve my goal. So bugger off – and watch me fly through my recovery.'

To me, this is the definition of resilience: giving life a crack, notwithstanding pain or failure.

LIFE LESSONS

Riding high on success, I discovered that it was a long way to the bottom when my Olympic dreams shattered. When failure hits, how do you cope?

* Understand that failure is often not your fault. It's not that you didn't try hard enough or didn't tick all the boxes. Sometimes it is just not meant to be.

* Failure doesn't mean that your sacrifice wasn't worth it. The lessons you learn can be your success.

* How you deal with failure will determine your happiness. Feel it, accept it, mourn it and then use it to fuel your future goals.

The punches keep coming

> **When life throws you curveballs, count your blessings. Avoid focusing on what you cannot change and try to be a blessing to others.**
>
> **Jackie Pittman**
> *(My best advocate and world's greatest mum)*
>
>
> **When the going gets tough, the tough get going.**
>
> **Brian Pittman**
> *(My dad, my hero)*

I told you there was a happy ending ... and I promise you we'll get there, but not before a little more heartache, which I must share with you to paint the full picture. So please bear with me: I need to complete the story, as out of all of this came my success and self-acceptance. But this took several years for me to learn – and a couple more setbacks.

Finding a new path

One of the great things that came out of my Olympic heartache was that I realised I had put all my eggs in one basket. I know many people believe that to be successful, particularly in sport, it must be an all-or-nothing approach, but I feel this can be dangerous. When there is no buffer or other area to find joy in, and your singular goal is derailed, it can feel devastatingly dark. So, after London, when it was clear my days in athletics were numbered, I sat down and wrote a list of all the different things I could be. I used all that anger and passion to find bigger and better targets. I figured that if I had several balls in the air, one would land safely.

Sadly, soon after the Beijing loss, my marriage also fell apart. There were a multitude of reasons why this happened. As we all know, it takes two to tango – and we were completely out of step. We tried to rekindle it a few times, even renewed our vows at one point, but we were fundamentally wrong. It really hurt; it still does, to be honest. I might have not been successful at the Olympics, but failing in my marriage is still one of the things that can legitimately make my heart pang. Regardless, athletics was over, and I had my gorgeous little son to consider, too. The sponsorship dollars were fast drying up, so I needed a solid plan, and quickly.

I listed all the things I wanted to divert my passion towards, including finding another sport to enjoy. I promptly started cycling, rowing and boxing. There was a business idea on my list, perhaps becoming a gym trainer, so I completed a personal training course and considered opening 'Pitt Fit'. Speaking gigs started to fill my calendar and a job coaching kids at a school popped up. I was busy, but didn't feel like I was quite on the right path yet.

> **I sat down and wrote a list of all the different things I could be. I used all that anger and passion to find bigger and better targets. I figured that if I had several balls in the air, one would land safely.**

I had parked myself in one of my favourite cafés in Melbourne, Book Talk. Staring out the window while I devoured their famous banoffee pie, I overheard another coffee lover talk about sitting the medical entrance exam to become a doctor. Well, that was fortuitous. Light bulbs started flashing in my brain, my heart racing as the obvious dawned on me: becoming a doctor was the one goal I had coveted since I was a child, parallel to being an athlete. I had let it slip by the wayside as my sporting prowess had dominated, but I had always flirted with the idea of retaking that pathway when the time was right.

Over the years I had kept in touch with university, doing a subject here and there to keep my toe in the water. I had dabbled in a few midwifery subjects, already keen on the idea of women's health, as well as psychology, trying to understand the complexities behind the way we think. I'd never adequately undertaken the practical components of the courses, as I would be whisked away to compete overseas for months at a time. But now that running was off the cards, what was I waiting for?

I immediately booked my seat for the next annual medical entrance exam, which is a prerequisite for anyone wanting to study undergraduate medicine in Australia. The results of this exam are combined with your resumé, an interview and your other university marks or school results. I had heard it was tough, so I enrolled in one of those courses to help take the sting out of its bite. I poured all the passion and Olympic disappointment into perfecting the odd little number sequences and logical reasoning questions that would present themselves in the exam.

The exam was held at the racetrack in Caulfield, a short drive from my house in Melbourne. I knew I was good at holding my nerve when it counted on the track, but this was a whole different ball game. My stomach was in knots as I lined up with all the other thousands of hopeful medical students. Once I was in my seat and we were told to begin the three-hour exam, I went blank – nothing. I tried mindful breathing – still nothing.

My brain had exited and was off hanging with the fairies. For sport this is great, your mind checks out and lets the body do the work without you overthinking the outcome. But right now, I needed my brain to focus and bring home the academic gold! I tried hard to switch on, rereading the first question at least four times. *Get a grip, Pittman.* This meant so much to me, but my new plan of studying medicine was backfiring!

Finally, I snapped out of dreamland and raced through the questions: some were simple and the answer obvious, but for others I had literally no idea – it may as well have been in another language. The exam was in three parts, and you only had an hour for each, after which you couldn't turn back to the previous section. After losing time at the beginning and spending too much time on the tricky questions, the bell signalled the end of section one. I had at least seven questions left out of about 44 ... crap! The incomplete questions were lost. I attacked the remaining two sections with all I had, finishing them comfortably. If only I could sneak a look at the beginning! I hoped my guesses were lucky ones.

Every day I checked my email for the exam results. I had already been to Sydney and checked out both the University of New South Wales and University of Western Sydney, my first two choices. It was all so exciting. It filled my heart with such joy to think I might be walking around these buildings next year on my way to becoming a doctor.

I'd wake up, the wave of nerves would hit, I'd reach for my phone – nothing. It was agonising. This went on for at least three weeks till finally, on 19 September, the email arrived: 'Your results are available.' With trembling fingers, I opened my computer, logged in … and my results flashed on the screen.

Losing the Olympics had been hard – and my marriage breakdown had been shocking – but this took the cake. In my mind, medicine was the answer to restoring faith in my own ability. Conquering a long-coveted goal – becoming a doctor – would take the heat out of the Olympic failure. Therefore, the terrible exam scores boldly blaring at me signalled defeat. Another one.

The hits keep rolling in

The hits kept coming: around the time I failed the entrance exam, my ex-husband also met his future wife – and any hopes of reconciliation completely dissolved. I had dabbled in the dating game, too, but still held a flame for Chris that was hard to extinguish.

Nevertheless, one night I dragged myself out to a footy game in Melbourne; I had VIP tickets and a few of my friends were keen to be wined and dined. That was the night I met Carlo, one of the kindest and most gentle men I have ever known. We clicked instantly, mostly because he was such a large character that I could be silent and almost hide behind his energy. His enigmatic smile could light up a room.

Carlo was very special: he had *Alopecia universalis*, meaning not a single hair on his whole body. You would think that having been teased as a kid he'd hold a grudge, but Carlo had the most fantastic attitude towards life. One day when I was getting my hair done, he walked in, sat in the chair beside mine, turned to the young hairdresser and declared with a grin, 'My turn!' Completely stumped, the girl went bright red. He was always the joker; it was very refreshing. He reminded me to get on with life. Yes, there had been a few tough years, but it's all about attitude. It was my choice if I wanted to move on or not. He was also exceptionally patient with my behaviour as, despite my desire to move forward, I spent a lot of time living in the past and every five minutes I would throw a barrier up and sabotage our chances.

After a few months of dating, I was out for a run around the Tan, my favourite park jogging track in Melbourne. Sprinting up the Anderson Street hill usually makes me feel electric, but on this day I felt overwhelming fatigue. I was dizzy and lightheaded. I sat down on a park bench near the Shrine of Remembrance to catch my breath.

The last time I felt like this, I was pregnant. Noooo, I couldn't be, surely not! I was on contraception and usually very careful, but I had missed a few pills when I was travelling to a friend's wedding. I pulled out my phone and checked the dates, and realised my period was late. (I'd been training intensely for rowing, and hard exercise had a history of playing havoc with my menstrual cycle, so I'd put it down to that.) A few days later, the sore boobs had kicked in. I snuck out to the chemist for a pregnancy test, dashed home and shakily peed on the stick. The wait wasn't agonising because the two red lines indicating I was with child popped up instantly. *Oh dear.*

I promptly went for another hard run: *What the hell am I going to do?* Carlo and I were just starting to get into a nice comfortable groove, he'd just moved in … but a baby, was that something we were ready for? He was a wonderful father figure for Cornelis. Now it seemed we would have a child of our own.

The hard part was, I had been pregnant a second time a few years earlier when I was still married to Chris, and we had lost that pregnancy. So, my feelings were mixed; the pain of that miscarriage had been horrible, mainly because I had battled alone, telling only one friend and not even telling Chris until many years later. I now thoroughly believe women need to share their pregnancies with loved ones earlier: yes, it's terrible if a miscarriage occurs, but that's when we need support.

So here I was, pregnant for the third time, and my mind flitted from complete fear to elation. I waited a few days to tell Carlo, petrified he would break off our relationship. Part of me wanted to will away the pregnancy and I even looked at options for termination. I am pro-choice, but for me it wasn't a path I could take. It would haunt me, as I had always wanted five kids and I am a little fatalistic. Was this the sign for us to become a permanent couple? A real future, together.

Finally, I sat Carlo down and told him, 'I know this is far from ideal, but I think I am pregnant.' The enormous grin and bear-like hug he gave me removed all my fear. His reaction was perfect, and I settled into a new happiness after a year of disappointment. A few weeks later we told our close friends over dinner, and I really started picturing Cornelis, now five, holding his little brother or sister.

Loss

A few days later I woke up late, fatigue still battling with my normal sprightliness, and headed to the bathroom. I noticed a small smear of blood. I screamed for Carlo, who came rushing upstairs, and I broke down in his arms. He put me to bed and we spoke to the doctor who told us there was nothing we could do at this stage but wait, hopeful that it was a one off. I did the usual Dr Google and tried to find examples of bleeds and successful pregnancies. Why, why was more pain being pushed into my life? What was I doing wrong? That night I prayed to every god I could think of.

Sadly, the next day the bleeding became torrential and a blood test a week later confirmed we had lost our baby. My second miscarriage. My guilt raged too – had I willed the pregnancy away, had I trained too hard, was it my fault?

Naturally, Carlo was devastated, but the serial optimist said, 'Well, it wasn't meant to be. Want to try again?' This time we actively planned to fall pregnant and had a lot of fun doing so.

We didn't have to wait long. After one cycle, the stick clearly showed two bright red lines again! Joy filled my heart and I had never hugged Carlo so hard. I was incredibly excited about this new little person cocooned in my belly, albeit the size of a sesame seed. We promptly went and bought a tiny little pink dress. We knew the risks but wanted to put good energy into the universe so that this little tacker would make it.

It was time for our first scan. There, on screen, was our little seed, just a blob; a flickering little heartbeat. What a relief! Carlo was over the moon with excitement, too. The sonographer checked a few things and said it looked good, although the heart rate was a little slow … but it was early. She advised us to come back in a week, just as a precaution.

We had decided that it would be better to move to Sydney where my parents were, so they could help us with our budding family. Carlo had a job interview up there, so would miss the next scan, but we thought it was just a formality. We had seen our little seed last week anyway. I climbed up onto the bed and the sonographer applied the customary ultrasound gel before placing the cold probe over my lower abdomen. She found the blob straight away ... but it wasn't flickering! She tried several different directions, even an internal vaginal ultrasound, but she didn't have to tell me. I knew our little seed had died. He or she was gone. Nothing can prepare you for this loss. Even writing this 12 years later, tears well up in my eyes for what could have been. All my hopes and dreams for this baby shattered. I felt bereft and so alone.

Crying is not a weakness but a healing strategy, a normal human way to deal with heartache. Sure, it is not for everyone, but it was my release valve.

Numb, I walked out to the car and just sat there. I called Mum first, as I didn't have the heart to tell Carlo. I felt so confused. Had we tried again too soon? Was there something physically wrong with Carlo or me? After all, I'd lost Chris's baby, too. Maybe all the years of sport had left me broken in more ways than I'd thought.

I had no answers – and, really, it was pointless looking for them. I will never know why, but the fact remained I had lost yet another baby. My third miscarriage.

The hardest part was that I didn't show signs of miscarriage at all. I sat around for a week waiting for the bleeding to start, but nothing happened. I ended up having a curette procedure. It all felt surreal. After the curette, I started bleeding so heavily that maxi pads couldn't help the situation, so Mum bought me maternity pads; the irony was not lost on me.

Worse still, I had continued with a few of my university subjects and had to sit an exam while I was haemorrhaging. I remember sitting down in the back row of the exam hall, as close to the toilets as possible. Would you believe, this day of all days, the adjudicator who gave me my paper was heavily pregnant? It took all my strength to hold back the tears. Halfway through the exam I felt another gush and tried desperately to get the woman's attention for a leave pass to the bathroom, but it was too late; I had made a mess of myself, and my indignity could not be hidden. Nor my pain.

In deep

I hadn't realised I had been treading water for the past few months or, honestly, the past few years. I now slipped into the deep end. The following 12 months became the greatest psychological battle I have had to withstand so far; the closest I got to giving up and throwing in the towel. My usual 'find another goal – come on, give it a crack' attitude was smothered in defeat. Even chocolate tasted bitter!

My family rallied around me, as they always do. My friends could see I was struggling and booked regular visits to help me with Cornelis, but my grief was a heavy cloud that took months to budge. Carlo and I tried to continue our relationship, but I was horrible to him, so hurt by life that I couldn't face his beautiful smile and positivity, even though he too was hurting dreadfully. Things had shifted fundamentally. Anyone who goes through the loss of a pregnancy will know what I mean. On top of the previous years, I am surprised I made it through. I was also in my phase of 'don't cry – suck it up, princess'. I'll discuss this more in the chapter called Enough, but, in short, I had been heavily criticised in the media for being too emotional and dramatic, so had decided to rein myself in. It had been working, so I thought, as I had managed not to shed a single tear for several years. Now I look back at that and realise it was totally ridiculous, and even a little bit sad. I was so busy trying to fit in with others' expectations, I was failing to care for myself. Crying is not a weakness but a healing strategy, a normal human way to deal with heartache. Sure, it is not for everyone, but it was my release valve, and without it I was slowly combusting.

Now there was *so much* heartache to endure. It was time to re-evaluate. Was I doing something fundamentally wrong? Or could I hang on to the hope that my luck was due to change? Either way, it was time to take a few big steps towards sorting my life out again.

I often get asked if my drive and resilience are innate or learned. Are some people just naturally more driven, or is it possible to teach someone to toughen up, push harder, heal faster?

As you know, I am all about 'you doing you', so I don't want you to learn to toughen up – I prefer that you find ways to value yourself just the way you are. Build on your strengths, rather than quash your weaknesses. To me, resilience is not the ability to withstand hardship, but to push yourself out of your comfort zone, even when everything in you says, 'Hold up, don't do it, stay safe.' It's the ability to stare fear and doubt in the face and do it anyway. Let yourself fail and then recover afterwards, on repeat. Use your varied experiences as an opportunity to examine your motives and rebuild into a stronger, more content person. Only then will you take the risks that will likely lead to even greater success.

LIFE LESSONS

True success in life can only come with self-acceptance.

* Take stock of where you are at: how are your dreams changing as your circumstances change?

* Roll with the punches.

* Let yourself feel; let yourself cry. It can be cathartic.

Phoenix rising

> **The principle of success derives from a place deeper than the surface level of mere accolades. Amid the major setbacks and challenges of life, one can constantly push to be the best version of oneself. It is this foundation that allows for success to repeat and renew in all aspects of life.**
>
> **Melinda Gainsford Taylor**
> *(Commonwealth champion and 100m Aussie record holder)*

I was debating my next move. One day, my little son Cornelis, who was then around six years old, sent a paper aeroplane down the stairs. On it was a picture he had drawn of himself and me playing in a park, just a few stick figures and shrubs, but what was clear were the big dark drops he had drawn falling from my eyes and the words he had scribbled: '*I luv you mum.*' Remember I hadn't cried, I hadn't given myself permission to cry, so how did this six-year-old boy know his mummy was in so much pain?

The result was an opening of the floodgates. I cried for days: all the frustration and doubt poured out and Cornelis just cuddled me and said, 'It's okay, Mum, even the sky cries sometimes.' A quote I now love, one he had obviously been taught at school. It touched my heart so deeply, I swelled with pride, and my gratitude overflowed that I had birthed this little treasure, that I was his mum. My greatest success was standing right in front of me! That little light-bulb moment reignited the fire in my belly. It was only a little spark at first, but I realised two things: firstly that it felt better to let out the pain – bottling it up and carrying it round like a ball and chain was such a heavy burden – and secondly, my son needed his mother back.

Destiny

So no, I never went on to win the Olympic Games. That was not my destiny. Yes, my marriage failed, and so did several other relationships. No, I have not got over the babies I lost: I carry that pain every day, even now as a mother of six. I had several other setbacks too: a cervical cancer scare, horrible media shenanigans, battling with an eating disorder and some very serious financial stress that had my kids and me eating baked beans on toast for almost a year.

> **I realised two things: firstly that it felt better to let out the pain – bottling it up and carrying it round like a ball and chain was such a heavy burden.**

None of us set out to fail. Very few of us would start a task if there was a guaranteed loss. Therefore, when things don't go to plan the discomfort is inevitable. I think one thing many of us do is run away from that pain. Squash it down, bottle it up, lock it away and avoid doing things like it again. As I did. This avoidance strategy works for a time, but as life inevitably throws you more and more curveballs, it leaves you with a whole lot of high defensive walls and only a short ladder.

Use the pain

I made a conscious choice to use the pain and not be afraid to fail. I had been there, I was okay with it. Don't get me wrong: my inner critic still exists, but I just listen patiently and then continue anyway.

A year had passed since I had failed the medical entrance exam and, in my head, I was very nervous about opening that can of worms again. What if it proved for a second time that I was just too dumb? Mum called me up the day before the registration closed to sit the exam. She wasn't gentle in her encouragement and pointed out that I had absolutely nothing to lose. So, I registered.

I booked to sit my second exam in Sydney, but due to unforeseen circumstances I had to fly up from Melbourne to do it. My session was in the afternoon and I had booked an early morning flight, giving me plenty of time to get to Homebush and relax before the exam. It was funny having the exam within a stone's throw of the Olympic stadium. Again, bad luck struck. There was a thick fog, which grounded all flights. I sat at Tullamarine Airport for three hours, slowly growing more and more anxious. I even called the Australian Council for Educational Research (ACER), who run the exam, but they said there was nothing they could do. If I missed it, I would have to wait another year. I couldn't change venues either.

Finally, the airport loudspeaker announced the plane would be boarding and my heart leapt into my mouth. I landed in Sydney only 35 minutes before the start of the exam. I escaped off the plane and ran so fast through the airport, I think I broke the 100 metre world record with my hair flying and bags flapping like a mad woman. Luckily, people just stepped out of my way. I left my overnight bag there. I was going to make that exam.

I hailed a cab and offered the driver $100 extra to cover any fines if he got me there in 20 minutes. He was a great sport and we sped along, flying through the traffic; the red-light gods were on our side. I landed at the exam entrance with three minutes to spare. I slid into my seat, still huffing and puffing, as they told us to begin the three-hour exam.

> **How you proceed depends on your attitude: it is just a mind shift. The only person who can stop you, is you.**

After it was done, just like the previous year I waited impatiently, checking my email every 10 minutes for the results. I was out shopping when the answer popped up in my inbox. I raced home to the privacy of my house. It took me a long time to open the file, because I was so afraid of the outcome. Finally, I did ... and there, staring back at me, was a big fat 97th percentile! I screamed so loudly I am surprised the police didn't come to investigate. I rang my parents and they must have thought someone had died, as through my tears of joy I could not get a word out. Soon they were crying, too. I had passed with flying colours.

In one solitary moment of bravery, every single thing changed. All my opinions about myself, my fears, my anxiety about not being good enough, the pain from my failed marriage, the loss of my babies, and the injuries … everything evaporated. I had a future. A real one! I was going to be a doctor, and no-one could take that away.

Victory after defeat

So, it worked, and this single victory cemented my idea that we have a choice as to how we use our failures. We can try to avoid heartache, but at times life will still deal devastating blows, some of them far worse than others. How you proceed depends on your attitude: it is just a mind shift. The only person who can stop you, is you.

So, take your life journey by the reins and write your own future. It doesn't matter how many chapters it takes, or how often you fail, as these just prove you have a strong and resilient emotional armour. The only way you lose is if you stop trying.

Importantly, though, when you make it out of a dark place you have a choice: to squash that pain and never relive it, block it away, close that chapter weighted by the anxiety it causes. Or, here is a thought, why don't you consider putting it on a pedestal and shining a light on it. Use it to prove how terrific you are at living through your own internal war. This is the greatest kind of success, yet so many of us see those times as a failure.

Feel the pain, get angry with the injustice, and then rise like a phoenix from the ashes.

LIFE LESSONS

My key to getting through hardship is simple: survive one day at a time. Every day, go for a walk and find one flower or bird that makes you realise you are alive and progressing. Hindsight is an amazing thing, isn't it? It took me many years to realise that the best way to build stoicism is to live through setbacks. I have learned more from my failures than from all the success and happiness I have achieved.

* No-one sets out to fail, but your attitude to the failures and setbacks can make a difference.

* Listen to your inner critic, then go ahead and do it anyway.

* Shine a spotlight on your failure and use it to light the way ahead.

A risk worth taking

> You must use yourself as your inspiration. Believe in the process. When I am fit enough, I can get fast enough; when I am fast enough, I can win. You don't need someone screaming at you to work harder, you need to love what you do, so that the effort is more enjoyable.
>
> **Sally Pearson**
> *(Olympic 100 m hurdles gold medallist)*

Medical school was amazing. Having failed the entrance exam the first time but then having the courage to sit it again almost made the whole thing sweeter. It showed me that fighting for something you want is better than having it handed to you on a platter. I loved the daily grind of learning about the human body, delving into the chemistry of pharmacy (medicines), exploring various diseases and the crazy cascade of inflammation. Every day my mind absorbed more and more amazing bits of information ... with awe. Our bodies are remarkable. As I moved into clinical medicine, sitting with patients and hearing first-hand about their life and illness was a private privilege only few get to experience. Progressing through the years, I moved from being a spectator into being involved in the actual surgeries. Initially there was a buzz at just being allowed to hold a retractor or close the skin sutures, but lately I have been passed the blade and labelled the primary surgeon.

I am truly humbled and in love with my medical career. I still pinch myself every day that this is my future. I also 100 per cent believe that if I had won at the Olympic Games in athletics, I would not have been looking for another opportunity like this and would likely have settled into a coaching or TV career and not become a doctor. That failure was my greatest blessing.

A change of course

It wasn't only medicine I had decided to take a risk on; I really wanted to make the Olympics in another sport, to be able to change how I felt about the Five Rings and my history with them. I was still rowing and boxing, but then, out of the blue, I received a phone call from Astrid Radjenovic (formerly Loch-Wilkinson). We had trained together many years earlier under Jackie Byrnes, but then Astrid had moved into bobsled. She was inquiring if I would consider joining her and bidding for the Winter Olympics. Well, why not? What an opportunity!

If I had won at the Olympic Games in athletics, I would not have been looking for another opportunity like this and would likely have settled into a coaching or TV career and not become a doctor.

The fear set in: *What if you aren't good enough, what if you get hurt, will you have time for your medical studies?* I sat down, closed my eyes and pictured the worst-case scenario: I imagined I was somewhere in Europe at an ice track (like I'd seen in *Cool Runnings*, the movie about the Jamaican bobsled team). I imagined Astrid and I were pushing the sled out from the top, crashing badly and failing to make the Olympics. I then fast-forwarded my imagination to failing an exam because I had put too many hours into training, all a waste.

I opened my eyes and reasoned with that imagery. The conclusion I came to was, 'Well, I can repeat a year of medicine – what is a year? – and I get to slide in a bobsled: who gets to do that, right?' It was a good, calculated risk with little consequence. Besides, being a winter sport with the competition season overseas mainly in our university holidays, it wouldn't interfere with my studies much anyway. I signed up.

Baptism of fire and ice

Holy cow, it was freezing! To an Aussie, this was a different world. Stunningly gorgeous snow-capped mountains, but the bitter coldness soaked through to your bones. I landed in Germany just after Christmas 2012, and little did I know that Astrid had picked the most dangerous and feared sliding track for my introduction to bobsledding: Altenberg. It would be a baptism of fire!

We competed in the two-woman bobsled. Astrid was the pilot who drove the sled down the icy slopes, and she was hoping I would be the brakeman, the big muscle on the back who got the sled off to a fast and fierce start.

The first time we pushed the sled off from the top, we went gently: *Aaahhh … ooohhh … mmmyyy … ggoddd*. I felt like I was in a giant washing machine. I held on so tightly my knuckles were white for hours. It was horrible: bumpy, scary and plain revolting. My head was spinning as we got out at the bottom. Astrid was clever and didn't have a spare brakeman there, so I couldn't say no to a second run. I put on a brave face and off we went again. She told me to relax. She was right: this time I let my body flow with the sled rather than fight against it. With each run the fear seeped away and was replaced with an exhilaration that is hard to explain. The speed and intensity, coupled with slight danger, made for a heady and exciting concoction.

> **I let my body flow with the sled rather than fight against it. With each run the fear seeped away and was replaced with an exhilaration that is hard to explain.**

The track in Altenberg has a 320 degree turn called a 'Kreisel'. It is roughly halfway down the mountain, around the tenth turn. On one particular run, we set off, this time giving a proper push at the top. Oh, this was fun, the adrenalin rush irreplaceable. Astrid was having a good run, too: we were going fast, really blisteringly fast. Into the Kreisel we went, Astrid driving us up and down through the pressure created by the steep corners in the ice. It is so tight, the gravity pushes down on your back like a giant elephant has camped there. Just as we were about to enter the straight, something went amiss. Before I knew it, the bumpy sensation under me disappeared. Everything went quiet, until … *bam*! We crashed onto our side, my helmet hitting the ice. From that point on, everything was a blur. You hold on with whatever you have, but there are no seat belts, so it's just you gripping some 1-centimetre-thick steel bars next to the pilot's seat and wedging your feet into whatever you can find. There isn't even an actual seat, just a spot where your bum rests in the basic frame.

My body started to lift out of the sled, my shoulder now riding along the ice. The sled often doesn't stop till the very bottom, or sometimes it stops at the bottom and then the momentum carries it partway back up the track, the sled behaving like a pendulum until it finds its final resting place. Eventually, our sled stopped, and Astrid popped her head up to see if I was okay. The pilot can slide in under the main hull of the bobsled, so often it's the brakeman who cops much of the brunt of any crash or problem on the ice.

> *I was a natural at bobsled: in athletics my size had always been a hindrance and I'd been on a constant diet (that became disordered eating at times), but in bobsled my beastliness was an asset!*

After all my injuries in athletics, do you think I was injured, participating in one of the most dangerous sports in the world? Nope. Absolutely nothing wrong except that I broke a nail. Hilarious! I didn't even have a good ice burn to show for it. It was awesome! In fact, for my whole bobsled career I was injury free ... crazy, really. I was hooked: this sport was perfect for me. Astrid was amazing and it quickly became apparent we were going to make a good team.

Over the following weeks, we raced in different places around Europe. It was quite full on. Not just the training and racing – the sled took hours to prepare. It was a big hunk of metal weighing 340 kilograms with Astrid and me included. Just lifting it was a challenge! Between sessions it needed to be carefully maintained: it had to be oiled and the runners sanded till they were like mirrors. Most days we would be up early, loading and preparing the sled before we spent about four hours at the top of a snowy mountain waiting for our turn to slide down the ice. I was a natural at bobsled: in athletics my size had always been a hindrance and I'd been on a constant diet (that became disordered eating at times), but in bobsled my beastliness was an asset! My fear about not being good enough to make the transition to winter sport quickly evaporated, replaced with excitement about becoming the first Aussie female to make both a Summer and Winter Olympic Games.

My son Cornelis travelled with me for parts of the season, bringing with him his little kiddie sled. It was a great adventure and a true highlight of my life. When he wasn't with me he stayed with my amazing mother, my rock. All my life my mother has been there, silently holding me up; without her unwavering backbone, I wouldn't have the success I do. That is one aspect of my life that I try hard not to take for granted.

Olympic success

Soon the Sochi Winter Olympic Games were upon us. The Australian team comprised a small group of 60 athletes covering all the different sports. This meant we cheered each other on avidly. Despite being in different sports, many of us shared a gym coach: John Marsden worked regularly with my fellow Olympians – Chumpy, Sami, Holly, Steph, John, Jarryd and Belle. I felt like I belonged to a family.

I had thought I would never experience an Olympics again, but here I was. It was honestly perfect. I tried to slow it all down and capture memories on my internal camera, consciously taking in every minute detail, savouring the moment for life. I barely remember my Summer Olympic experiences – they are all a blur – so this time I wanted to suck in everything I could, slow it down and really appreciate the amazing opportunity I had been given. Again, one that would not have happened had I been victorious in athletics.

Race day came swiftly and soon we were slipping into our sleek, one-piece green-and-gold suits, slamming on our helmets, donning our gloves, and whacking the hell out of our matching green-and-gold Aussie bobsled. It was magnificent. Of course I was nervous, but at the start of the race I took a moment to absorb it all and be grateful. A second chance at elite sport: I couldn't have been luckier.

We pushed hard from the top. Once the sled started moving faster than our legs, Astrid jumped in and a few steps later I leapt in behind her. All I had to do then was tuck my head between my knees and hold on. The sliding is really all about the pilot: she is the finesse, I am the brute strength.

We flew through the corners, tapped a few walls, but mostly they were quite clean runs. At the bottom I pulled on the brake, a metal lever with teeth that eat into the ice, stopping us just past the finish line. Climbing out, we were dizzy with excitement. I was officially a dual-sport Olympian.

It was honestly perfect. I tried to slow it all down and capture memories on my internal camera, consciously taking in every minute detail, savouring the moment.

We finished in fourteenth place overall. For a country with little snow, a small budget and no bobsled facilities, this was a brilliant result. I can, hand on my heart, say it was the best Olympic experience I have ever had. I missed the closing ceremony, as I had to fly home early for the start of the university term; however, I will never forget the wonderful experience I had in Sochi. The risk was worth it!

Being your own advocate is easier said than done. Taking a risk is worth it, if you can get over the fear of failure and ensure it's a calculated choice. I always advise anyone who is facing a big decision in life, to sit in silence and picture the worst-case scenario. Really try to feel what that would look like … experience the anxiety and stress. Could you live with that outcome? If not, perhaps you need to change course; your fear mechanism may genuinely be trying to protect you. If you can find a way to live with the potential failure, then go for it!

LIFE LESSONS

When you're faced with a risky opportunity, take a moment to imagine the worst-case scenario. Can you live with the failure?

* Success after failure is all the sweeter; it makes you appreciate it more.

* Unexpected twists in the track can upset the smooth running of your life, and you sometimes have no choice but to try again.

* Make sure you're present in the moment: it's not always all about the result.

Enough

> **Success is completely within your control when you realise that you allow, promote and create everything that happens to you. I learnt to take ownership the moment I realised that my biggest weaknesses were my greatest opportunities for improvement, if I wanted to achieve my goals.**
>
> **Melissa Wu**
> *(Olympic and Commonwealth diving medallist)*

This is a chapter that is very close to my heart. What is 'enough'? For me, this word takes on so many meanings and innuendos. Is there ever enough happiness, love or freedom in the world? On the other hand, the idea of heartache gives rise to the well-used phrase, 'I have had enough'. And it crops up in my self-reflective mind chatter: 'Am I good enough?'

It all relates to the measure of having just the right amount of something ... enough, but not too much. Not many words have such a strong, personal impact for me as 'enough'. It sums up this book: to me the greatest success in life is believing in yourself – accepting that you are perfect just the way you are.

Today I'm able to look in the mirror and feel perfectly imperfect and, finally, 'enough', although it took a lot of work to get to this point. I am now far more comfortable in my own skin, but that self-acceptance came after many years of inner debate, and is still a work in progress. I am by no means an expert: I am just an Aussie girl who has always been a big dreamer, a hard worker, and a bit of a 'pit bull' when it comes to attacking a goal. I also acquired a touch of good luck, mostly because I found my village of people who have stood, steadfast, alongside this quirky, sensitive and dramatic soul.

Drama Jana

One of the hardest parts of being a public figure is that your life is never private. So, along with dealing with sporting or relationship setbacks on a personal level, I had to hear everyone else's opinion on my downfalls, too.

While nowadays most journalists are wonderfully complimentary about my life, and my name is often linked with kind terms like 'lioness' or 'wonder woman', there was a time when the headlines made even my mother cringe and led me to regularly question who I was. As those who are old enough may remember, I was infamously known as 'Drama Jana'. I used to tell myself, 'Don't worry, Jana, today's news is tomorrow's kitty litter', but in truth I was putting on a brave face and the comments often cut deep. As they kept coming, my self-belief often wavered and there were times I hated myself for being different and too emotional.

I am not sure I *was* very dramatic. Incredibly passionate, and overly emotional, 100 per cent yes. But creating drama ... not as much. I can still hear my mother's curt, yet somehow gentle, voice telling me, 'Enough is enough, Jana,' as she tried to hose down some emotional jaunt I had embarked on. I am apparently what's called an 'empath', someone who is prone to intense emotion but also recognises those feelings more quickly in others. I cry when I am happy, sad, hungry, in love, and don't get me started on a romantic movie! It is also likely why I love being a doctor, where my patients can be the focus of my intensity. But did I create extra drama? I think not. I had enough real 'crap' going on that I didn't need to become melodramatic about extra things. In fact, I am proud of how I handled all the ups and downs of my sports career, especially considering how often the Olympic Gold seemed within my grasp but slipped through my fingers. I also regularly joke with my mum that if my name was something other than Jana (and therefore didn't rhyme with drama), maybe I'd have been 'Heroic Helen' or 'Mighty Michelle' … but that's not the case.

As you read the remainder of this chapter, please don't think I am still made sad by the media. Gosh, at times it had me questioning every cell in my body; however, in hindsight, as a more mature woman and when 90 per cent of my media coverage is now beautifully positive, I look back at that harsher chapter with gratitude. As always, I look for a silver lining.

As a result of some of the negative media, I am not afraid of speaking freely about lots of taboo topics that need to be openly discussed. People now say, 'Oh, that's just Jana; we love that she's an open book and authentic.' I instigate conversations around incontinence, vaginal discharge, Pap smears (now called cervical screening tests) breast health, mental health and miscarriage. I post very real pictures of my body post-pregnancy on social media, share when the kids have nits, rarely wear make-up and happily jump around in my Modibodi period pants.

Even more importantly, I openly talk about how I once tried to change who I was in order to be more accepted by the public, more palatable to others, and how I lost who I was in the process. I have the privilege now of using my story to help others reflect on their own personalities. Examine what you think needs changing and then question it. We are all uniquely beautiful in our own skins.

Media maven

As a young up-and-coming star in athletics, there were many occasions I was grossly overpublicised: all I had to do was wear new shoes and someone found it newsworthy. My life in the public eye started when I was only 13 years old, with our local rag coming to my school for a quick picture and story of my teenage sporting escapades. I did this very awkward pose in my Parramatta Little Athletics two-piece, one leg propped on a tree, so much gel in my short hair that the wind couldn't budge it. Mum used to collect all the now faded clippings in a giant grey manila folder, until they became so numerous that they filled several shoe boxes, then a filing cabinet. These days the stories are mostly published only online, but she still holds on to the magazine articles, particularly the ones in which I am the journalist writing on women's health.

To this day, I am not sure why I drew this attention. It started to become a mixed bag of positive and negative press around the same time as my injuries derailed my Athens Olympic campaign. Therefore, let's start with the Athens debacle, and I will walk you through my media journey and how it impacted my self-belief.

As you may recall, I was the odds-on favourite to win gold at the Olympics when I suffered a devastating injury just weeks before the opening ceremony. The media had a field day with my downfall, following me and my support team around as we tried to sort out treatment options. They camped outside our hotel room, bombarded us at the airport and were waiting for me at the hospital after my knee surgery. In fact, if I had to pinpoint a particular event where the media went from loving to caning me, I think it was the crutches incident.

> **I love that the world now seems to be gravitating towards accepting the person behind the image that the lens has captured.**

After having my operation in London, I walked out of the hospital to a waiting throng of media. The surgery had been so successful, I no longer needed the crutches that I had relied on to carry me into the hospital only 24 hours earlier. So, I tossed them aside – *How amazing is this? When you get told you can't, defy the odds and prove that you can* – as I was trying to show that a minor miracle had occurred and to inspire hope.

The bulbs flashed big time. I thought I had created a hero story showing what we Aussies can do, but sadly it was a time when reality TV was not yet in favour and I was mercilessly criticised for my dramatic hospital exit.

I genuinely think that these days people would have seen it as a bit of fun; they would have laughed and enjoyed the realness of my story. I love that the world now seems to be gravitating towards accepting the person *behind* the image that the lens has captured. However, at this time, it was the start of a media storm and the first occasion that I was labelled Drama Jana.

It continued when we joined the other Australians in Italy at a holding camp, where I had amazing medical support to continue the post-surgery progress. Someone had tipped off the media, so we also had a swag of extra attention focused on our every move. Neither Phil nor I could predict the saturation of stories that flooded the Aussie papers; and we were also two very positive humans who could only see the remarkable side of the past week. As a result, Phil allowed the media to join us in recovery sessions. He figured they would take the footage anyway, over a hedge or through a window, so we may as well befriend them and have a little control over what was produced. Or so we thought ...

Over the course of the week, we became good friends with the two cameramen who rallied with us, one from Channel Nine, my sponsor, and one from Channel Seven, the station with coverage rights to the Olympics; but little did we know of the station war that was happening at home. From all accounts it was a little like a prelude to the Kardashians: my life was featured as a soap opera across everyone's television screens, as the stations fought to be first with the latest update.

My parents were in Athens already, and the local television stations only showed stories on Greek athletes; and my brother was in Afghanistan. If we had known what was going on, I am sure Phil would have canned all the sessions and found a more private setting as, realistically, I was also recovering from surgery, incredibly nervous about the Olympics and feeling the pressure immensely. We just didn't know.

I dissolved into tears, devastated by the result and rightly so: I was the reigning world champion and hadn't been beaten in months.

When we arrived in Athens it was insane. The media scrambled and pushed each other out of the way to get their shot or shout out questions. It was a circus. After each race, I tried to stay positive and gracious in my interviews. I was proud of how I handled the intense questioning. When I didn't win in the final, I praised Fani Halkia, who had won my event in her home country, just like Cathy Freeman had done at the Sydney 2000 Olympic Games. I truly thought I had been a good role model.

What we didn't see was that the cameras followed us back to the private 'no media zone' at the warm-up track, where Phil was waiting for me after we lost the final. I dissolved into tears, devastated by the result and rightly so: I was the reigning world champion and hadn't been beaten in months. If I hadn't been disappointed by my injury and loss, I would have needed my head examined. It was supposed to be an intensely private moment. A TV camera had snuck into the area and was filming me at my most vulnerable, only to replay my agony for people back home, fuelling public opinion that I was emotional and dramatic.

From this point on, for several weeks, the media turned very sour and the headlines replayed my failure, repeatedly, although really it was a minor miracle that we had even made it to the start line, let alone the final. People were even going as far as saying that I'd never had the operation and it was all for show. My sporting life was in tatters and my reputation was being torn to shreds

Within the week we boarded the Qantas charter flight home. A plane full of Olympic athletes. Crazy! I have no idea why, but they gave me a seat in business class with all the Olympic medallists. Everyone else rode cattle class. I am sure it was meant to be supportive, but I had to sit with the athletes who truly deserved it, pulling out their medals and relaxing in their triumph. It made me acutely aware that I had failed in my quest.

The plane landed in Sydney and pulled into a private hangar where friends, family and the media were waiting for our arrival. Those seated up front were first off the plane. I spotted Mum instantly and made a beeline for a cuddle. The media swarmed around us, but now the questions were more about what I thought of my new tag, Drama Jana, and whether it hurt that my nation no longer liked me. Even this was apparently a story. What questions to ask a 21-year-old with very little insight into the situation. I tried to explain we didn't have any idea, but that only made it worse. I would have given anything to have someone gently say, 'Shhhhh Jana, say nothing.'

I do look back now and think it is funny that people thought I sought out the media, aimed to be in the spotlight. The stories were often quite negative – no-one in their right mind would want or go looking for that.

At that day's post-Athens parade, the crowd was overwhelming and you could feel their excitement.

After seeing our family, we were ferried to Sydney Harbour to do the ticker-tape parade. This is a wonderful event where you walk from Circular Quay down one of the main streets of Sydney as you wave at the crowd. I remember doing it after the Commonwealth Games in Manchester when I had won. I just loved it. Giving high fives to the kids, signing autographs and taking pictures. A chance to mingle with the public and show appreciation for their support. It was marvellous fun.

At that day's post-Athens parade, the crowd was overwhelming and you could feel the buzz of their excitement. They waved Aussie flags, shouted out to get our attention and were chuffed if we waved and smiled. The energy was electric.

Just as we were approaching the Town Hall a man walked up to our group, smiling. As he got closer, he recognised me and promptly spat in my face, before denouncing me: 'You are a disgrace to this country.' Shocked, I pulled away as a few people around him laughed, joining in with his excitement. I tried to hold back the tears, but it was clear I was struggling, only to have another group of people close by call out, 'You going to cry again, Jana? At least you are good at that.'

We were called over to assemble on the stage and be presented to the public. I kept my eyes fixed on the gorgeous blue sky above us and recaptured my composure. 'It is not their fault, Jana, they don't know you,' I repeated to myself, like a mantra.

Finally, I found my parents and escaped to their house. I didn't tell them anything. I just went straight to the cupboard, found a hidden block of chocolate, and wolfed it down.

Love–hate relationship

The media events of 2004 were the start of a love–hate relationship with the media. It was expensive competing for your country, so you needed sponsors, who insisted on media exposure. Therefore, I was caught between a rock and hard place. If I did too much media, I was labelled 'media hungry'; if I did too little, I couldn't afford to take my physio with me to Europe. We all know my injury history, so that was not an option. It meant that every interview I did, I was afraid of saying or doing the wrong thing. It was the start of me changing who I was … I could hear the rehearsed lines flowing from my mouth. I hated it, but it was safe. I tried to keep my guard up and refused to discuss anything topical in case it was misconstrued. I also had a select few journalists who I trusted completely to do stories if news broke. Oddly, though, even when we said no to media, stories broke about me, regardless, without my comments. There were a mix of positive and negative stories about injuries, training with the Geelong footy club, several charity things, new sponsor promotions and more.

One string of articles really hurt both me and a fellow athlete, Tamsyn Lewis. We had always been good mates and she had supported me during Athens when everything had gone pear-shaped. She was the last person I would want to alienate. A silly joke by Tamsyn on the radio about beating me, meant entirely for fun, was fuelled up into a totally ridiculous feud that didn't exist. I was young, and in hindsight I can't believe I read and took the media stories as gospel, especially when

I knew how incongruent they could be. I believed the stupid hype, which cost us our friendship. Years later we mended things, but it was never the same. In a sport where only a few athletes are elite enough to compete internationally, it can be a lonely road, and I missed her deeply.

A few weeks out from the Commonwealth Games in Melbourne I was feeling quite confident with my campaign. I had overcome a few injuries, which of course had been played out in the press as, 'is this going to be a Drama Jana Athens repeat?' We ignored this and I was firing on all cylinders over the hurdles. Feeling brilliant and ready to bring home gold for Australia.

A new journo asked me to contribute to a story she was writing. She told me she wanted to write a feel-good fluff piece leading into the Games about some of the heroes in athletics. I dropped my guard and agreed, loving the idea of being a 'hero'. We met over a coffee and the interview went smoothly. In fact, it was great fun. She was hilarious and seemingly kind, sharing about herself like we were old mates. I walked away feeling I had made a new friend – in fact, I had invited her to come out for dinner with a few other friends the following week. Then she wrote one of the most hurtful articles ever written about me. It basically claimed I wasn't a proud Aussie, didn't enjoy running for my country anymore and was ditching Australia all together. A traitor to my nation.

I rang her and asked why she did it. Her response was, 'It's nothing personal, it's just media.' She wanted to build her career on my downfall, and her article continued to fuel the 'drama' fire and hurt me deeply. Not only did it cost me two major sponsorship contracts, but my self-confidence took yet another hit.

> **Some people care little for other people's friendship, while others, like me, crave acceptance. For a long time I thought the fact that I looked to others for validation was also one of my faults.**

What I never understood is how sports people can inspire young kids to take a better path in life. As a doctor now, and mum of a teenager, I see how kids with no dreams or plans can make poor decisions, often out of boredom or because they are in with a bad bunch. Journalists have the power to create heroes for our kids: they can promote role models to keep them on track or inspire them to say no to drugs or other dangerous activities. So why break us down and beat us up?

Sure, some athletes (like all of us) make mistakes, say silly things, get into trouble and will get bad press. As far as I am aware, that wasn't me in a public setting. I won bucketloads of races; I tried to smile as much as I could; I was generous and forthcoming with my time and opinions (too much so at times); and I tried hard to be respectful of others and see their ideas and point of view. But on many occasions as a young athlete, I just couldn't seem to say or do the right thing. I was just never enough.

Find the way out

Why did I care about the meaningless stories? Why did I second-guess everything about myself and try to fundamentally change who I was? For years I vowed never to cry or show vulnerability. Why? Because I was a kid who desperately wanted to be liked. It is just the cloth I was cut from. Some people care little for other people's friendship, while others, like me, crave acceptance. For a long time I thought the fact that I looked to others for validation was also one of my faults. It's not one of my best traits, but it is one I have learned to accept in myself and check in with regularly – to reassure myself that I am worthy whether this person values me or not.

It got to a point when I decided to be that cardboard cut-out, cereal-box athlete. I thought that if I subdued myself I would be happier and more well-liked by the public. My self-worth was tied to my popularity. So I said no to countless media opportunities, prepared my statements and asked for editorial approval for any stories, plastered positive quotes all over my house and put up a huge front to the world – one of pure strength and no emotion. I appeared bulletproof and impenetrable. In truth I was like a duck in a rainstorm: calm on the surface but paddling like mad to stay afloat.

It worked for a while, until the energy required to keep up the ruse became a burden. Not to mention the fact that I started focusing so much on the 'opinions' of others it became almost a fixation, a tireless quest to be 'enough'. But enough for who? I was left feeling absolutely destroyed on the inside; so fake. And – guess what? – I failed way more: my eating disorder reared its ugly head; my marriage got worse and worse; and the sporting injuries became more frequent. It's crazy that your body can't overtly tell physical stress from mental stress, and mine was on overload. No wonder it broke down more often.

I grew angrier and sadder, but refused to let it out, refused to show my weakness, refused to be dramatic and emotional, refused to be me. I smiled despite the pain and hated myself deeply. Several truly heartbreaking things happened during this period, such as the disintegration of my marriage and the multiple miscarriages, but even then, I faked my courage. I was numb.

Until the day when my own little boy snapped me out of it with his simple but perfectly timed cuddle and picture. Don't get me wrong, it still took another four or five years until I could genuinely look in the mirror and love the woman staring back at me.

I spent oodles of time sorting through my mental baggage and looking at who I was and who I wanted to be. I wanted to be proud of who I was, respectful of my failures and become a dream chaser again. I wanted to be able to tackle frightening things and run head first at tricky challenges. Why? To me that is what life is about.

I came to realise my emotions are my secret weapon and I should not have been squashing them.

My intensity returned and with it my passion. I know these things can be offputting to others, but they make me who I am. It is also what makes me emotional, as I fall head over heels in love with a new goal and then get all crazily invested in it. I get teary with excitement when I conceive an idea, then cry happily when it starts to move in the right direction and again when I achieve it. On the flip side, if it fails, I also have torrential tears; it's a wonder I am not dehydrated! I let all the pain out. I cry for as long as I need to, till one day the pain is less and I am ready for the next door to open. My heart is free to genuinely take on a new opportunity.

So, in fact, I guess I haven't really grown up. As kids, when things don't go to plan, we scream our lungs out and the next minute we are onto the next thing, the loss long forgotten. Why do we not do that as adults? Sure, we have more responsibilities, and some pain can't be relieved by a good cry – but it can help! I came to realise my emotions are my secret weapon and that I should not have been squashing them.

My intensity, my overt passion and my emotion were the main three things I didn't like about myself. These same three things, which I thought made me weak, turned out to be the foundations of my resilience.

Find your resilience

I know I am not alone. Being hurt can greatly affect how we feel about ourselves. It can go as far as it did with me, and make you really question who you are. Just remember that no-one can hurt you unless you let them. Think about your self-perceived flaws and inadequacies: are they really as bad as you think? Or are they, too, part of your success story? If so, perhaps trying to accept them is a better option than trying to overcome them. Easier said than done, but once we acknowledge our own quirky differences, others will likely accept them too. I tried to change who I was in order to fit in, but it backfired. I feel lucky that I identified it before I completely self-destructed. By accepting differences, I found I was more content with life. I still love being liked, but it doesn't define my self-worth. People will either like me for me, or they won't. I am enough.

LIFE LESSONS

The thing I want you to remember about this chapter is that it's exhausting trying to be someone that you're not, just so others will like you. It is also time consuming, and this energy could be directed positively towards achieving your goals.

* My battles with the media show that the way you are perceived by others can be very different to your own reality.

* Hold on to your true self; value your 'weaknesses' as well as your strengths.

* Having other people like you is less important than learning to like yourself.

Cut the fat

> What's the best way to eat an elephant? One bite at a time! This saying reminds me that big things are achieved by doing little things every day. It's not so much about being motivated, but about being consistent. The small bites add up.
>
> **Turia Pitt**
> (Bestselling author, podcaster and running coach)

I was back on the set of *SAS Australia*. The helicopter lifted slowly off the ground, sending clouds of dirt swirling away from the blades. I fastened my seatbelt and gazed across to the rugged DS Ant Middleton. He was taking me in, trying to ascertain if this middle-aged mum was going to succeed, fail at the task or, worse, chicken out altogether. We flew out over the lake and hovered about 20 metres above the cold water below. Ant turned to me and reiterated the plan. Climb out the open door, lower yourself onto the makeshift monkey bars (just a ladder that lay across the legs of the flying metal bird) and hang there. Then, one rung at a time, hand over hand, traverse to the other side until you reach the last rung a metre beyond the width of the helicopter. Turn around. Swing your legs up, secure yourself and climb back into the helicopter. Don't fall off or you will drop 20 metres and hit the water hard.

> **I had already watched several other recruits lose their grip and enter the water below in spectacular fashion.**

Right! All while the pilot was keeping the bird flying; the water spraying up as the power of the helicopter created havoc on the surface of the lake; the rotating blades whirring loudly above; the wind swirling in all directions; and my hands slippery with sweat. Yet, despite all the noise and chaos, I could still hear my heart thudding in my chest and feel the fear rippling up and down my spine. It was beyond crazy: it was wild and exciting.

I did exactly as I was told, almost slipping off right at the start, as I lowered my 85 kilogram body – which only five and a half months previously had birthed my fourth child – onto the monkey bars. The rungs cut into my fingers as I slowly made my way along the metal ladder treads. One rung at a time, right hand, left hand, right hand, left hand. *Come on, keep going.* I had already watched several other recruits lose their grip and enter the water below in spectacular fashion, limping out winded and sore. *Please not me; come on, Jana.*

Left, right, left, right. I reached the end. Now to turn around, which required me to swing my wrist backwards at a terribly unusual right angle, then expect it to take my full weight while the other hand also reoriented my body to face the open helicopter door. *Go! Ahhhh, so close!* My fingers slipped, but somehow I managed to regain the grip. I could now see Ant again, gesturing for me to hurry up and swing my body back up onto the ladder and climb in next to him. But how? My stomach muscles did not exist: I had an abdominal separation left over from the pregnancy and this skill would require a huge ab crunch and a pull-up to get me moving. I had nothing to lose, so I swung hard. And missed. I swung and crunched even harder and missed again. *Come on, third time lucky, you have got this!*

I closed my eyes and considered my options. Fall and get wet, or keep trying. Eventually my grip would fail so, till then, swing, swing, swing. Several more attempts and I could see this was futile. I noticed the side of the helicopter was in reach of my feet if I did a small pull-up through my arms and then thrust my legs out. Giving everything, I kicked my legs out wildly and landed a foot on the side of the helicopter, then wrenched my body upwards till I was almost hugging the ladder. Then my foot slipped back off the side and I was once again hanging from the bars.

It's so easy to be distracted by the environment that we forget we already have the weapons we need to conquer the challenge.

This was crazy. The helicopter started moving around even more, the noise was deafening, and I was losing heart. By now I had been holding the weight of my body through my arms for five minutes. The muscles were aching and tiring fast. *No, no, no. I am not going to fail this. Come on Jana, use your heart. Give it another go.*

I took a deep breath, and somewhere deep inside me a little voice coaxed, 'Cut the fat, Jana: if you take away the noise, the hunky man and the helicopter, it's just monkey bars in the gym!' Correct. I had done this before in the gym, repeatedly. I gained momentum by swinging backwards and forwards, then planted my foot hard against the helicopter. I wrapped the other leg around the ladder to ensure that this time I couldn't slip back. Then, gripping madly, I inched my body up around the side of the ladder and, suddenly, it was over. I had done it. Climbing back into my seat, shaking with adrenalin and excitement, I couldn't wipe the smile off my face.

To me, this is the perfect analogy for so many things in life. We need to remove the distractions, stop overthinking things and just get on with it. In other words, it's so easy to be distracted by the environment that we forget we already have the weapons we need to conquer the challenge. Remove the unneeded inputs and keep focused. This is my go-to now, but it didn't happen overnight, it took practice. I learned to identify the things that would sabotage my success, and narrow down to the essentials the tools that could make the road easier to navigate.

The reframing tool

In 2012, I knew my inner chatter had become quite sabotaging. I was still good at shutting it off during a race or under pressure, but my daily self-talk wasn't doing my confidence any favours. It had got to a point where I was berating myself left, right and centre for silly stuff, such as saying the wrong thing, laughing too loud, or worrying about an unfinished task. I lost sleep over future outcomes and people's opinions. All useless. All a distraction from what I wanted to achieve.

So, it had to change, and it did. I actively worked on retuning my inner dialogue. I was working with a great guy called Jamie, who gave me back the 'elastic band' strategy that I had used as a young athlete but had shelved many years ago. It's a simple theory: you wear a band on your wrist and flick it when your mental chatter goes in a direction that doesn't serve a purpose. For example, when a negative media comment makes me feel terrible about who I am, I immediately flick the band and replace the thought with something positive, such as, 'But, Jana, you are an amazing mum.' Do this enough times and your brain starts to rewire. It requires commitment; it takes a while before you interrupt your thoughts early enough to shut the negative ones off. For me, now, it has become an automatic thing. I still have negative thoughts regularly, but I don't need the band anymore. I just say *no* and replace that thought with something productive. I catch myself being my own worst critic and tell that unwelcome voice to move on.

At the same time as I started wearing my elastic band, I also finally gave myself permission to feel sad about setbacks. I watched movies like *The Notebook* to keep the tears rolling and allowed myself to sit with the pain from so many years of heartache. After which, feeling quite refreshed, I started cracking on with new goals, passionately starting to chase after new ideas.

All my intensity returned in full force. I knew I might still suffer judgement for my strong personality traits, but I was far happier being me, no longer worrying about someone else's opinion. Flick, flick, flick of the band. It was such a release.

I said yes as often as I could to daunting opportunities – such as bobsled. I built up courage to take the medical entrance exam again. I sought out new friends, especially people who had similar big ideas. I started doing more speaking gigs, which initially I sucked at, often feeling like an imposter on the stage. However, with time, they reinforced my own message to myself: it's okay not to be okay, and you already have what it takes to succeed.

> **I still have negative thoughts regularly, but I just replace that thought with something productive. I catch myself being my own worst critic and tell that unwelcome voice to move on.**

Interestingly the saying 'success breeds success' rings true for me, just like using failure as a weapon to refuel a goal. I feel that having the mental flexibility to look at both situations and remain positive is key. So, when you fail, let the pain come pouring out and then use it to push on; but, when you succeed, celebrate wholeheartedly, as that will give you more confidence to continue on the path. It's a combo of both. Ultimately it just means we aren't afraid to have a crack – and if we fail, we have the resilience to cope with it.

As the final stage of accepting myself as I am, I stepped right out of my comfort zone. I had been asked to do many TV and print media biographical interviews over the years, but I was always too afraid of being judged harshly by the public, too distracted by the external perception to consider the opportunity. I argued that most reality shows have a villain, and I was sure to be cast as that character. So, agreeing to do *SAS Australia* and *Australian Story* in 2021 took a lot of band-flicking for me to get past my insecurities. I was already a doctor by then, and really loved my life in medicine, so did I want to rock my very comfortable boat?

I hadn't changed; I was still the kid who dreamed too big and spoke too fast, but somehow it seemed the world had grown to like the realness of a fallible fable.

I was still battling with that fear right up until the minute they put us on the *SAS* trucks and the cameras started rolling. But it was perfect, as that opportunity epitomised everything I now choose to stand for.

I had come a long way since my sporting days. I needed to show myself I was no longer afraid to be myself and that my worth was not guided by public opinion or media. That I was okay, just the way I was. And that's exactly the way I want you to feel, reading this.

So, I cried on national TV, wore my heart on my sleeve and talked openly about peeing myself and how much I missed the kids. As a recently reminted mother, having just given birth to my fourth child, I kicked goals because I refused to give up. I showed I was competitive in the boxing fight, openly afraid of heights, a gumby on the balance bar, but intelligent with my memory and unashamedly proud of my flaws.

Interestingly, in this show it was my overt emotion – the realness and vulnerability that, when I was a young athlete, had been seen as a negative – which saw me praised as being authentic and honest. I hadn't changed; I was still the kid who dreamed too big and spoke too fast, but somehow it seemed the world had grown to like the realness of a fallible fable.

Take back control

Perhaps you are reading this and agreeing with me that you want to take control back, cut away the unnecessary noise and be more self-accepting of who you are. The next big question is how? Of course, it is different for everyone. Spending time working out what clicks for you is worth the investment. You must also identify what things are out of your control and not worth losing sleep over.

I have six kids and a mortgage, so whether I like it or not, I must earn an income. Being a stay-at-home mum would be wonderful – it would remove my terrible mother guilt – but it simply is not an option. So, when the maternal pang comes, I reframe it. I say to myself: 'I love my kids and I love my job; we are happy, healthy and thriving. Hush now, heart, you've got this.'

Ultimately the greatest distraction in life for most people is the incessant noise in our heads, the inner dialogue we have with ourselves. It can be your greatest ally but, for most of us, it can also get in the way. It is all well and good saying, 'I am going to be kinder to myself', 'From today onwards, I will like myself' or 'Tomorrow I will not be distracted by my phone.' But living that truth is not that easy, is it? It takes time and a persistent effort on our behalf to catch ourselves when we aren't keeping our own promises.

LIFE LESSONS

If, like me, you have had things or people in your life who have brought you down and made you second-guess your worth, remember that you have the tools to reframe your life. Flick, flick, flick.

* Be yourself, accept who you are and lead by example.

* Stay on task, be aware of potential distractions and enjoy the uncertainty of life.

* Hush that inner saboteur and celebrate your wins.

Ownership

> **A big part of taking ownership is being able to critique your own performance. It's about finding solutions rather than focusing on the failures. I take ownership of my life by setting lofty goals. Once my goals are determined, it's all about consistently putting my plan into action each day, until I've reached my desired outcome.**
>
> **Kerri Pottharst**
> *(Olympic beach volleyball gold medallist)*

I have heaps of flaws. I am fabulously human after all. So I talk too fast. At times don't listen enough. Care too much. Cry too often. Drive too fast – yes, this is a very bad choice and now I must drive super-carefully as I only have two points left on my licence. I often eat too much and then have the same regrets we all do as the bloating sets in and the cramps disturb my evening. I regularly work too hard and take on too much, which heightens my raging mother guilt and adds to sleepless nights. I worry about all my wrinkles and my messy hair, but forget to moisturise and have no idea where my hairdryer is.

As you know, I am all about accepting yourself for who you are, but I also think being aware of your quirks can make the road a little smoother. Owning your choices and flaws doesn't mean putting yourself down, it opens you up to accepting who you are and being aware of the things that might challenge you. I am still a work in progress, learning about what makes me tick and overcoming my insecurities, but I want to share a few of the issues I had, and the way I came to understand and deal with them, which might help you on your journey.

Find your village

I am incredibly time poor. I am always asked about how I balance my life – my simple answer is that I don't. If you want help fitting in a hundred million things at once, I am your woman; but if it's about finding a sweet life structure with ample time for self, close the book now – I am not the person for you. In fact, this is one of my lifelong flaws. My restless legs, which are currently shaking the table right now, have always itched to go places. While this characteristic is great for kicking goals, it needs to be kept in check.

As you know, I was the queen of the nerds at school. With my desperate desire to be liked, I really struggled when people weren't keen to befriend me. But how could they? I was so busy training and studying, I was so laser-focused, I didn't allocate time to give friendships room to grow. On the flip side, had I been a social butterfly I probably wouldn't have had the early success I enjoyed in sport. It's quite the social sacrifice. So, my early awkwardness was really a blessing, but a lonely one.

> ***I was putting so much energy into sport and keeping up appearances in public, that I almost lost what really mattered.***

I am incredibly grateful that I now have a steadfast village of like-minded people. We advocate for each other, hold up a mirror when needed and love unconditionally. One of these amazing people has stood alongside me since the age of nine and, despite my intensity, so have a few of my other wonderful mates from high school. Still more joined my circle from the fields of sport and medicine. We are a small, quirky bunch, but true friendship is worth its weight in gold.

However, there was a time when I could have lost many of these friendships. I was so caught up in my own life and desire to win at the Olympics that these friendships were running on the smell of an oily rag. Too many unanswered phone calls and emails made me a poor friend – which is ironic, given I was so keen to be accepted myself. I was putting so much energy into sport and keeping up appearances in public, that I almost lost what really mattered: my village.

One night I went to a party with a group of friends. Most of the evening was spent rehashing previous activities and life events they had all been a part of, but I hadn't; often because I had been off racing or chasing some other goal. However, some of the memories they discussed I could easily have been part of – but I had not been invited along. I sat there quietly taking it all in and feeling very lonely. I realised it was my fault, as I had not invested the time to ensure these beautiful people felt valued. I had said no so often that they just assumed I was too busy or uninterested. I had to own this: this was totally my doing and I had to fix it.

I am so grateful for that night. It taught me several things. That success is wonderful, but not if you have no-one to share it with. Also that no matter how busy or tired you are, there must be time set aside for the things you value. Having friends is very high on my values list. So, I worked extremely hard to reignite my friendships and, gosh, it was worth it when the tough times arrived and they rallied behind me. They picked me up and carried me through. Although my friendships are often the type where we don't speak for ages but can always pick up where we left off, I needed to ensure that my friends felt as heard and as appreciated as they made me feel.

Scratching the itch

One of my other flaws, which I think affected my overall sporting outcomes, was impatience, which caused me to swap coaches too often. In hindsight, I can see that I always had itchy feet and loved to change things up. Therefore, despite having some of the world's best coaches over the two decades I competed for Australia, I moved around too much. I blamed my 'elite athlete mindset': pushing for more, the extra one per cent. This excuse holds some truth, but, really, any of my coaches could have taken me to the top of the Olympic podium.

As a very young athlete I started off with Mrs Mac, Wayne Clarke and Charles Tees, then when Jackie Byrnes approached me to train with Melinda Gainsford Taylor, my excitement swiftly took me into her squad. Fira Dvoskina joined hands with Jackie as my hurdles coach, and together they took me on to winning three junior world titles and getting my first Olympic berth. Then the lure of the Australian Institute of Sport came calling and I moved to Canberra, to be trained by the amazing Craig Hilliard. Under his keen eye I won my first Commonwealth Games title. Then the great Phil

King approached me to move to Melbourne and train with him and Roy Boyd; they had collectively coached Phil's wife, Debbie Flintoff-King, to win gold at the Seoul 1988 Olympic Games in my event. 'Wow,' I thought, 'what an opportunity!' So I moved again, and we won my first senior world title in Paris in 2003 together.

Thinking the grass is greener and constantly changing things up was not the way to build a strong base. Growing together, learning from and about each other, and fostering trust would have been a better way forward.

Then came some devastating injuries in the Athens Olympics – both Phil and I felt heavy-hearted about this and needed a break, so Chris, my future husband, suggested I come and train with his squad under Nick Dakin in the United Kingdom. This sounded like a wild adventure, so off I went. Chris ended up becoming my coach himself, a challenging mix for anyone let alone an emotive athlete like me. Chris and I won my second Commonwealth title and second world title together. Sadly, our marriage didn't outlast the turmoil of yet more injuries, and when we separated in early 2011, our coaching arrangement naturally dissolved. I went back to Phil King, riddled with injuries and lacking adequate focus, but we gave it another crack, which sadly fizzled, I believe largely due to unresolved issues (on my part anyway) stemming from the Athens Olympic campaign. Finally, I tried a few months with Peter Fitzgerald, John Quinn and Mike Hurst, but my heart was already in medicine, so the commitment wasn't adequate.

All these amazing people, these superstar coaches, gave me the world. All of them deserved to coach me for my career in its entirety. Why do I reflect on this as an issue, as I still won medals under all of them? Well, the truth is, we are all human and complex. I genuinely feel I would have been more successful in the Olympic arena if I had stopped and looked at the components that were an issue and addressed them. The outcomes may have been different. Thinking the grass is greener and constantly changing things up was not the way to build a strong base. Growing together, learning from and about each other, and fostering trust would have been a better way forward. I was responsible for the constant change. I made the decisions and it's important I own this.

As an older and, I hope, wiser woman, I am aware that this is an issue I continue to have, but now I question my reason for wanting to jump ship before I take the irrevocable leap. I still get the desire to drastically change career paths, but I now sit and reflect on whether it really serves my family and me. Then I try to choose more wisely. If I still feel restless, and the desire to have a big change continues to exist, then I find a trusted loved one and talk it through. This person is often my mother (over coffee and chocolate). We try to work out the underlying cause and deal with it, or at least plan for the path of least impact on those around me.

Learning to trust

One of my greatest flaws is an inability to trust. Particularly when it comes to partners and their love for me. I am a self-proclaimed expert in relationship failures, having been engaged five times but only making it to the altar twice. It sounds comical, reading this, but naturally it hurt, badly. I never had an issue falling in love, in fact it likely happened too quickly, but the relationships soon fell apart. I think several reasons existed for this. Firstly, I yet again listened to others' opinions too often, not really believing my own opinion was valid and never trusting that someone would pick me; always scared that when they really got to know me they would leave. Let me share a few of my disasters with you.

I fell heavily in love with Rohan Robinson. When I was a teen, he was the bee's knees in Australian athletics. At one stage I had a poster on my wall from when he competed in the Atlanta Olympic Games: a total fan girl. Never in my wildest dreams did I think he would become my partner! I had watched him compete for years. Then, suddenly, I was in the Olympic team and there he was, within reach. Over the next two years, I would flush red if he walked past or shiver if I brushed up against him in a bus en route to the track.

When I moved to the Australian Institute of Sport in Canberra, it was his squad I joined. So, for several months I followed him around the track like a bad smell. Giggling like a schoolgirl at his jokes and oversharing about life, trying hard to befriend him. It worked: after a while we became unusual mates despite the 10-year age gap. I just fell more heavily for him with every passing day. I am not sure when we crossed the line from friendship to lovers but, hand on heart, he was extraordinary.

> **If I still feel restless, and the desire to have a big change continues to exist, then I find a trusted loved one and talk it through.**

To distil time and words: he was one of the great loves of my life. I worshipped him. We moved in together and 18 months later we were engaged. Of all the relationships I have been in, we were the most compatible, but I listened to everyone else who kept trying to tell me our situation was flawed. They told me he was too old, they told me not to trust him and that he was bad news.

Eventually we broke up in a totally unexpected fashion, less than 24 hours after I won my first world title. We should have been celebrating but we had a stupid, small but explosive fight, and I ended things abruptly, not really thinking it was permanent.

> **I yet again listened to others' opinions too often, not really believing my own opinion was valid and never trusting that someone would pick me; always scared that when they really got to know me they would leave.**

We regularly had small tiffs like this: wasted energy that needed to go into the track. My coach Phil suggested that since it was less than 12 months until the Olympic Games, I needed to make sacrifices if I wanted to win; I had to focus on my running. I listened. I wouldn't say I regret it, as what is meant to be will be. If Rohan was The One, we would have reunited. However, for years I questioned my reasoning. I sadly then compared my next few relationships to Rohan, and he is hard to beat.

When I finally met Chris, his seductive British accent and athletic swagger made me weak at the knees. We did marry, and for a time were brilliantly happy. We had our gorgeous son together, and as Chris had an incredible eye for coaching, we enjoyed great success on the track, too. Sadly, he also had a whiplash response to my insecurities. When we met, I was confident and happy in my own skin, and he revelled in my affection, returning it with gusto. His radiant smile and wicked sense of humour were intoxicating. We met prior to any of the negative press, but soon we were embroiled in the height of my media shenanigans. As you know, I tried to keep a brave face, but behind closed doors I was loaded with self-doubt.

Sadly, Chris didn't understand why I was so sensitive, as he was unwavering in his self-belief. My crying was obnoxious to someone that confident and strong. In the dark times, we brought the worst out in each other. In fact, I am not sure which was the chicken or the egg: did our relationship cause stress that made me prone to injury, or did the injuries cause conflict that affected our marriage? Most likely it was a combination of both.

In his defence, it wasn't an easy time for him either: in the early days when I was winning medals all over the world, he was retiring, forced to stop athletics due to his own injuries. Not only did he have to sit by my side and smile through it, but he was also coaching me. In hindsight, perhaps he thought me a little useless not being able to control my emotions and get on with it. Maybe if we had stuck it out a little longer until I'd reached the life chapter where I switched off that side of myself, we might have worked. But then I am sure something else would have exploded. We just weren't a good match when the chips were down. I never felt enough for him. When our relationship ended, I was a blubbering mess and incredibly hurt. Something had broken deep inside of me.

> **I was so good at not letting past life experiences impact my future from a career perspective ... but when it came to intimate relationships I sucked at taking my own advice. I carried every failure into the next one.**

Then came Carlo, the kind and endearing, larger than life, bear of a man. I tried not to sabotage our potential, but I constantly pushed him away. He was so nice and seemed to care so much for me; but, still reeling from the pain of my divorce, I didn't feel deserving of that love. When we fell pregnant, I thought, *This is a sign, come on, Jana*. When we lost the babies, the walls I had built around my emotions doubled in size.

After that, I had four or five more relationships, including dating an incredible woman. I was engaged another two more times, but those relationships fell apart too. In hindsight, I realise I was terribly afraid of getting hurt. So I would choose a safe option, someone I didn't love, to avoid heartbreak, or refuse to let the good ones get close. I worried about family and public perceptions when it came to dating women, so blew those chances out of the water. I actively pursued a man who wanted me to give up my medical career and be a trophy wife, until that reality had me running for the hills. Then I almost married another guy who was wonderful to my kids, but didn't particularly like me. It was one comical disaster after another.

It is ironic really: I was so good at not letting past life experiences impact my future from a career perspective – throwing myself again and again at the Olympic podium – but when it came to intimate relationships I sucked at taking my own advice. I carried every failure into the next one. With each relationship demise it became more and more apparent that the only common denominator was me: I was the issue.

Just as with my other friendships, my lovers needed to feel valued and important. I was always jetting off to races, studying for the never-ending exams, heading to bed as the sun set, and I rarely had time to holiday. All that, combined with the heavy baggage I now carried from both my divorce and the media, made it tough for anyone to walk next to me.

Romantic movies have a lot to answer for when it comes to love. For those lucky ones who do find it, hats off: please write a book for all of us who don't. My parents have it, my brother has it too, along with lots of my friends, so I have seen proof it exists. I just don't think it exists for everyone.

The day I made the decision to find fulfilment as a solo woman was the day I finally felt free to walk a different path. It was so cathartic. I finally stopped chasing what I didn't have and accepted the opportunities in front of me. It started with the decision to have my girls, which will be the focus of the next chapter. It then changed the way I viewed potential partners. I took back ownership not only of my heart, but also of the mistakes I had made.

LIFE LESSONS

Accept yourself for who you are, but be aware of your quirks and personal battles. Owning your choices and flaws doesn't mean putting yourself down; it gives you the power to grow with them.

* Find your village and make sure they know how much you appreciate them.

* Take time to look before you leap into life-changing decisions, and consider the effects on those you love as well as on yourself.

* Learn lessons from your failures and own your responsibility for them.

My miracles

> Have an open mind: if a Good Idea that can benefit the people pops up, investigate it and never give up on the road to knowledge.
>
> **Mats Brännström**
> *(My hero: the first surgeon to facilitate a live birth after a uterine transplant)*

I was sitting in a practical skills session on taking bloods at Blacktown Hospital when my phone rang loudly, interrupting our tutor. I quickly excused myself, to her dismay, as this was it: the call I'd been waiting for. I knew the nurse on the other end of the phone would give me the news I craved so deeply. 'Morning, Jana, can you confirm your date of birth and address please,' she asked. I rattled off my details, my heart thumping hard. 'Well, Jana, I can confirm you are indeed pregnant. Congratulations!' My fumbly hands dropped the phone and I let out a shriek so loud it brought the other medical students out of the room to check whether I was dying. It was real! I had peed on a few home tests, so I knew it was a possibility, but after so many miscarriages I needed more proof. I was going to have a baby, but this time I was single.

Longing for motherhood

Above everything I have ever done, my greatest achievement is my family. Let me walk you through how I ended up as a mother of six and a half kids, mostly as a single parent, and all while I was either competing or studying to be a doctor.

You know the story of Cornelis, whose father is my ex-husband Chris, born in the middle of my sports career. He was the apple of my eye and I desperately wanted siblings for him. I love having a brother and really wanted Cor to have a similar lifelong friendship like that. It was a big driver in my decision. After several miscarriages and failed relationships, I was very much losing hope. I had one gorgeous child; I needed to accept my circumstances.

I was lucky. I was now in my second year of medical school and run off my feet trying to keep up with the younger students in their twenties, with off-the-chart IQs and brains like sponges. Combine that with our Olympic bobsled campaign and I was busy!

But every baby I cuddled, or new mum I saw pushing a pram, made my ovaries squeeze. Gosh, I wanted a baby so much!

> *I am going to have a baby ... by myself! It took several more months before I garnered the courage to talk to my family about it.*

I tried to distract myself, but right before the Olympics in Sochi, the craving grew stronger and stronger and stronger. In fact, I was lying awake one night in the Olympic village when an old memory from many years previously surfaced. I had met an incredible woman at an event I was involved in. It was, oddly, a swimming competition where we raced other athletes to raise money for charity. After I was obliterated in the pool, I caught sight of a woman playing with identical twin infants in the wading pool. They were adorable and she managed the pair with ease. It turned out she worked for my sponsor and was quite senior in the marketing team. I made the off-hand remark, 'You must have a great partner to help you with these little gems, with a tough job like that.' She told me that she was a solo parent and had used a sperm donor. She recalled how she had got to a point in her life when her body clock ticked but no man answered, so she did it by herself. What a hero.

My miracles

I sat bolt upright in my bed. *I am going to have a baby ... by myself!* It took several more months before I garnered the courage to talk to my family about it, but the idea clawed its way into my soul.

I finally worked up the bravery to speak to my mother about it. I was still living with my folks at the time, after moving from Melbourne to Sydney for medical school, so it was hard to find the right private moment. Finally, I bought two blocks of chocolate – one would not be enough – and asked her to have a coffee with me. Over the following few hours, I presented my case. 'Mum, you know I have a terrible track record with relationships, but I have always wanted lots of children. I am in my thirties now and, after the miscarriages, I worry if I wait, I will miss out.' I also ventured down the path of how hard my divorce and custody battles had been the first time around, and that rushing a relationship in order to have a child could end up in a similar, or worse situation.

Trying to rein in those useless thoughts, saying to myself, 'Stop overthinking it, Pittman.'

I could almost see the cogs moving inside her brain. Ultimately I think it helped that she had always wanted a big family, too, but had only my brother Ryan and me. Her own journey with childbearing meant she was open to supporting my ideas. Ryan had no children yet, so she also feared she would miss out on the noisy Christmas parties. It was a yes! So, we started to explore the process: there was no rush, but, as with most things in my life, it was not straightforward.

Complications

I went to my GP, had the prenatal blood tests, and got a referral to see a fertility specialist from IVF Australia. He suggested I should have a cervical screening test (the old 'Pap smear') since I was way over the due date. I got a call a week later informing me I had returned a positive result and could I please deliver myself to the doctor today. I was at university, but left all my things and ran shakily to my car. What was happening? I had just decided to have a baby and now I was sick!

The 45-minute drive to the doctor's was a blur. I can't remember waiting an hour in the surgery. All I recall is driving to my parents' house afterwards, where my son was waiting, and telling them I had grade III cervical dysplasia, one step away from cancer. As a medical student, I naturally spent the entire night playing Dr Google, trying to work out the prognosis. Of course, I went down the rabbit hole: *what if it is already advanced cancer and I must have a hysterectomy. I couldn't have a baby.* Then, trying to rein in those useless thoughts, saying to myself, 'Stop overthinking it, Pittman.' Flick, flick, flick of my metaphorical wristband.

The next step was a colposcopy to confirm the grading – it could be a false alarm. From here on, things happened very quickly. I had a biopsy done. Lying in your typical stirrup position, with a large, bright light focused on parts you wish could stay hidden ... it was painful. The doctor bluntly informed me the abnormal cells were obvious. I felt sick; my heart felt like a deflated soccer ball being kicked along the ground in front of me.

It was yet another lesson for me to quieten my mind and not jump ahead of myself.

Finally, the call came that would decide which fork in the road I was destined to take. I could barely squeak out my name, and I almost hung up before I was told the result – better not to know, to hold onto my dream of having another child for one day longer. The gravity of the fact that it could be life-threatening hadn't even taken hold yet. The nurse informed me she couldn't give me the results over the phone and asked me to see the doctor in person. I felt numb. This could only mean one thing: the results must be worse than expected.

My mother accompanied me. Sitting in the waiting room, I looked around at the cartoon pictures on the walls. I felt like I was drugged, and the carefully illustrated characters seemed to be closing in on me. It is funny what fear can do to you. Mum slipped me a

Tim Tam, but I had no appetite; I forgot I even had it in my hand until it melted all over my fingers.

Finally my name was called, and I followed the doctor into his room. I felt so small and vulnerable. As he flicked on his computer and looked up my results, I could feel the sweat build up on my palms; the chocolate sticky on my fingers; my hands shaking uncontrollably. He opened my file and, turning to me, he said, 'Right, Jana, you are lucky.'

After all the build-up, finally someone upstairs was smiling down on me. It wasn't cancer. It wasn't even grade III anymore; the diagnosis was reduced to grade II. I felt the oxygen finally reach my lungs. It's crazy, how we dwell on things and convince ourselves of the worst-case scenario. It was yet another lesson for me to quieten my mind and not jump ahead of myself.

The journey continues

After the cancer scare, I wanted to expedite the process. I still had no idea what had caused my previous miscarriages; I had also been told that not all donors allowed single mothers; others preferred women who were considering multiple children. So I swiftly put myself on the sperm donor waiting list. Soon after this, a few wonderful male friends offered to be my donor. I agreed to one and we did a cycle together. It wasn't successful, which in hindsight was probably for the best;

during the process I realised that in his ideal world we would become a family. He didn't live in Australia and it would have been difficult for me to leave the country. There were lots of other complicating factors too, but the idea of a possible custody battle served no-one. As daunting as it was to consider being a solo mum, I realised I couldn't use a known donor.

Finding my hero

The actual choosing of the anonymous donor was oddly scary. Thankfully, I had Mum right there by my side. The email arrived giving us access to the database: each time we opened a new file we knew they could potentially be the genetic father of my future children. There were details on their career, medical history, likes and dislikes. Their favourite foods and music interests. There was even a description of what they looked like and details about their family heritage. It finished with a note to the future parents and child. It was this letter that helped me choose my donor. 'Your parents love you and have gone to a lot of trouble to have you.'

He was my hero. These men go through a lot to be donors. They aren't paid and are only selected after multiple medical tests and counselling sessions. I never realised how much trouble they are prepared to go through, to give women like me this gift. Once Mum and I had picked him, I let the fertility centre know.

Fairly soon after, we started a process involving multiple daily injections, blood tests and ultrasounds. Your ovaries are literally on overdrive. In a non-IVF situation, usually only one egg each month matures and makes the journey into the womb for potential conception, but when you have fertility treatments like IVF, the ovaries are stimulated to produce more than a dozen eggs. You feel like an absolute pin cushion and your belly becomes bloated.

Since little Cor was now eight years old, and this quest was largely about expanding our family, Mum and I thought that he should be included in everything. He held my hand when I gave myself the shots, even pushing the medication in for me. He was such a little champion, making me keener than ever for a sibling for him.

I never realised how much trouble they are prepared to go through, to give women like me this gift.

Finally the ultrasound showed multiple follicles that were big enough to be removed. It's a small operation, but it holds so much hope and angst. Waiting for the egg retrieval felt like being in the call room at the Olympics. It's comical really: baby making is supposed to be fun, but I know for sure this method is not enjoyable. There were lots of other couples anxiously waiting their turn. We surreptitiously looked at each other.

This is when it really hit me. I was alone. Sure, Mum was with me, but that signposted to everyone I was solo. It was an odd sensation and the first time I would second-guess my courageous and daring decision.

I changed into my hospital gown before a nurse came and tucked me into a heated blanket to await my fate. I watched as a few hopeful women went before me, clutching blankets around them as they walked into the theatre and hopped up on the surgical bed.

The doctor told me he would write a number on my hand to tell me how many oocytes (eggs) he was able to retrieve. Throughout the week prior, apart from the daily injections, I also had an internal ultrasound every second day. These examinations involve a complete lack of privacy and I felt quite invaded – yet, every time, I felt I could be one step closer to that longed-for little bundle. After theatre, as the still unconscious women were rolled back to the recovery ward, I couldn't help but try and take a sneak peek at what number was written on their hands.

> **The magnitude of the huge world around us often shocks me.**

(As a footnote to this experience, a few months after this I was lucky to experience a day in a fertility clinic as a trainee doctor and watch the procedure I had undergone. It was such a long instrument that went in through the vagina and needled the ovaries, collecting the precious eggs, each only 100 micrometres in size. I watched one woman who sadly had no eggs at all. They tried so hard to find one. The heartache she would suffer on waking was hard to fathom.)

Finally it was my turn. The nurse stuck her head around the corner and asked if I was ready. I walked in and, as the women before me had done, hopped up on the bed. The anaesthetist sent me off to sleep.

Before I knew it, I was awake. A big '11' was circled on my right hand, even better than my first cycle of seven. Eleven little hopefuls! I was so happy, you couldn't wipe the smile off my face. Surely out of 11, one little guy would make it?

Then there was one

That night I tucked my son in to bed and sang him to sleep. He was growing so fast but still loved a lullaby. Then I went and sat outside. There was a giant full moon staring back at me. It was breathtaking that night. The magnitude of the huge world around us often shocks me. I relived the pain and heartache from the babies I'd lost, the failed first cycle, the loss of my relationships, and thought of the possibilities to come. I was going to do it all over again. This was the scariest journey of my life.

The next day the laboratory called with an egg update. I lost a few straight up; they just didn't fertilise. Two days later the remaining eight had become four; they were all just withering away. The clinic called the night before the scheduled transfer to tell me I had only one little B-grade embryo; the other three had not made it at all. I was devastated. They said it was up to me if I wanted to transfer the remaining embryo and that it would be a long shot. I most certainly wanted to give it a fighting chance, plus what did I have to lose – other than a bit of extra money? A baby is priceless.

The next day, Mum packed me into the car and off we went. This procedure is much quicker than the retrieval. You lie down and they literally just pop the egg inside you, then up you get with an embryo on board. It feels like you should lie down with your legs up but, apparently, the embryos do all the work on their own.

What did I have to lose – other than a bit of extra money? A baby is priceless.

Over the next two weeks, I decided to act like nothing special was going on. During the first cycle, I had literally stopped my life. No training, feet up, meditating around the clock, acupuncture, eating pineapple, wearing orange undies ... and all the quirky fallacies listed for fertility. You name it, I did it. This time, I trained normally, studied hard and ate my normal diet. I didn't want to get my hopes up, so now it was just up to my little bean and my body.

The day before my blood test, I had sore boobs and felt a little nauseous, but I thought this might be psychological. I decided to buy a home pregnancy test. I wanted to prepare myself for potentially sad news. I got home and peed on a stick ... and sat there, giddy with anticipation, sure it was going to be negative. As I watched, very faint double pink lines started to appear. I pulled the second test out of the box, and there it was again! My little bean had burrowed in.

I ran, crying and jumping up and down, to Mum, who squealed with delight. I passed her the stick, forgetting it was covered in pee, but she didn't care, she just jumped up and hugged me. 'Let's wait for the blood test to confirm.'

You know the answer to that: the call came through while I was at uni. I was on cloud nine all day, but nothing beat the smile on Cor's face when I told him. I put his hands on my belly and told him, 'A little bean has taken up a home in Mummy's belly and is trying to grow into a baby.' I knew it was a risk telling him early, as I might have miscarried again, but he had been part of the process from the beginning. Plus, I needed my family to support me in the event I lost this little bundle.

Meeting Emily

As the weeks ticked away, the reality that my beanie was hanging in there became my future. I opted for the harmony test, which is an early but accurate way to check for common chromosomal abnormalities. The results were perfect and we found out my bean was a SHE! All my wildest dreams had come true. A little baby girl, to complete my pigeon pair. I love the relationship I have with my mum and now I too would have my own little girl to share life with. I cried with such joy, as she was healthy and clearly on her way to being my daughter. My B-grade bean had become the greatest little fighter.

Finally, it was time to meet my miracle. Like most mums, I had pictured this for nine months, or really for years: the day you meet your child for the first time. It was a fairly quick labour, and soon I was reaching down and feeling her head starting to crown. I got to deliver her myself, pulling out my slippery little sausage; it was truly amazing. I yet again fell in love with birthing.

I counted her perfect fingers and toes. She had tiny, pursed, ruby red lips and a lovely little button nose. She had more hair than her brother had at birth, but it was the same dusty brown and, when she opened her eyes, pools of blue stared back at me. Emily ... I had been debating her name for months, but looking into her face I knew it was the right choice: my grandmother's name, my middle name and now hers.

She was my perfect little princess to match my little star who was patiently waiting outside to meet his new sister. My rainbow family of three!

LIFE LESSONS

I have realised that there is no point in waiting for the perfect time, place or partner to build your dreams. Your goal might not be related to having children, but whatever it is, chase it, exhaust all possibilities and find a way to bring it to life. I am my own hero, and you can be yours.

* Chase your dreams, even if circumstances are not ideal – they are worth it.

* Let your family and loved ones share your burdens and your happiness.

* Never, ever give up.

A rainbow family

> As a gay man and a new father, I realise that family isn't always about blood. To raise a family, it takes a village. Our village consists of people who are truly happy for our success; who support and encourage us in our struggles; and are there to console and help us in the difficult times. A rainbow family is the true definition of love, respect and acceptance.
>
> **Brad Foster**
> *(Friend and father of Maíli, my donor daughter)*

I thought I was done and my family complete, but when Emily was about six months old, that familiar pang for another baby fired up. Mum agreed that adding another little cherub to our brood was a great idea. Therefore, we started the whole process again. Would you believe, again I only had one embryo that made it to day five and transfer. Like her big sister, she was classed as a lower-grade embryo, but just as she is today, Jemima was stubborn and robust.

She kept me on my toes, though, as at my first ultrasound I was told there was no baby, that the gestational sac looked empty. She was declared a chemical pregnancy. Just as with a previous miscarriage, my bleeding didn't start, so I prepared for another curettage. My fertility specialist suggested one more scan to confirm. And there she was, just a flickering little heartbeat, and my love for her was instant.

My girls are the greatest gifts I have ever received. It took guts for me to do it solo. It took even more courage to openly share my journey with others. Initially when people asked who the father was, I avoided the question, or changed the subject when I got the inevitable comments about how I must have a great husband to do all that I do. Eventually I realised that I have the privilege of being their mum because I was brave enough to defy the odds. I learned not be afraid of others' opinions, and push past the fear of multiple miscarriages. It dawned on me that, yet again, all my past experiences, all the loss, all the failures and the heartache, have led me to be strong enough to do this solo.

Women's health

My cervical dysplasia did end up progressing to grade III, and only this year did I finally get the all clear. Thankfully now as a doctor specialising in women's health I am more informed. The silver lining from my early diagnosis was that I joined the Australian Cervical Cancer Foundation (ACCF), which aims to teach woman about cervical dysplasia and cancer and how to prevent the disease. I have now been their ambassador for more than five years, and one of my more memorable adventures was travelling with the ACCF to the Philippines. We screened hundreds of women who had never seen a doctor, let alone heard of cervical cancer, some of whom had advanced disease when I met them.

After my own experiences, I really want to help other woman achieve motherhood. In my fourth year of medical school, I was looking for some motivation to keep the torturous study hours up while managing three kids solo. My mother sent me an article about an amazing Swedish surgeon, Mats Brännström, who was doing uterus transplantation and had just achieved the first live birth. Yes, you heard correctly, Brännström and his team are taking the uterus from one woman and transplanting it into another who can't have children, due to problems with her own womb. Perhaps she has had cancer or a horrific bleed during labour that required a hysterectomy, or perhaps she was born without a uterus.

Even though I was just a medical student, I worked up the courage to email this world-leading surgeon to ask if perhaps I could do a medical elective with him and watch him in person. Thinking I would hear nothing, I was shocked when only five minutes later he responded, saying he was an avid athletics fan and if I was prepared to do a quick presentation on sport, he would let me come for a few weeks and watch him in action.

Again, another example of stepping out of your comfort zone: nothing ventured, nothing gained! Fast forward five years and I helped bring this science back to Australia. After many 'no's, and countless hours of ethics and funding applications, our team hope to start the first uterus transplant surgery in 2023. Just amazing!

A growing family

My eclectic family tree continued to expand. After someone had graciously donated his sperm to me, I decided to do my part. Initially, I donated eggs to a family who had gone through 10 years of infertility treatment and multiple miscarriages. I felt the woman's pain and wanted her to have the same happy ending as me. I did two further rounds of IVF for them and now they have a bubbly little boy.

A few months later, I was up on the Gold Coast visiting one of my lifelong friends, Brad, and his partner Hamish. I told them I was considering doing surrogacy or more egg donation and casually asked if they had considered becoming dads. Initially they fobbed off the question. A few days later I got the surprising call that they would like to open that discussion. Fast forward a few years and their daughter Maìli celebrated her third birthday, a few days before I celebrated my fortieth. I did not carry her – they had a different surrogate – but she is biologically my daughter. I am her Aunty Jana, and my kids call her their sister.

Jumping forward

In 2020, my second husband, Paul, entered my life. He is intelligent, very successful at his job, works hard (which I admire) and has a good sense of humour. Best of all he seems to like me for my quirks. He is an intensely private man and therefore I will not discuss much of our relationship in this book, as it is not just my story to tell. We have an unconventional relationship based entirely on friendship and an agreement to have a family. Mainly because, while I crave to be around people, Paul is comfortable in his own company.

> *We all need to find our place in the world.*

We also have very different and varying interests and pursue those on our own terms. The independence allows us to be individuals most of the time but rally together when needed. Yes, it is unconventional and what we have is different to most, but perfect for us. Next to my own father, he is also one of the most generous men in existence. I think if one of the kids needed a heart transplant, he would be open to giving them his: it's just his nature and upbringing.

We are incredibly lucky to have three beautiful children, Charlie and our twins Quinlan and Willow, whom we love dearly. Maybe our marriage won't be forever, but I can guarantee that our friendship will be, because it is honest, raw and real. Just like me.

This proves that you don't have to fit the mould to be happy. There are many different styles of relationships, just as there are many different types of people. We all need to find our place in the world. I have an ex-husband, a current husband, my girls have a donor dad, and I am a donor mum. My ex-husband has kids with his new wife and the girls' donor has also helped three other families become parents. Imagine trying to draw our family tree!

Family is what you make it. Mine includes my parents, Paul, Brad, Hamish, my brother and his wife, my best friends and all our kids. We are a mishmash brood of imperfection, but we all love each other dearly, albeit in different ways. We are the perfect rainbow family.

LIFE LESSONS

My life has never fitted into an ideal pattern: things rarely go as planned. I have learned to take the good and the bad and turn it into a new kind of positive reality. And mostly it feels like it's all turned out for the best.

* Find your village of family and friends and let them hold you up when the chips are down.

* Pay it forward: if you've benefited from someone's generosity of spirit, let others benefit from yours.

Leaving it with you

> Find a hero who has walked the path before you, someone who has proven your goals are possible. Every time you start to lose faith, take a moment to breathe and think of them and what they would do if they hit a barrier.
>
> Jana Pittman

My final key that has helped me navigate the bumpy road of my life has been to seek out people who proved that all my crazy ideas and goals were possible. Some of them I knew personally, such as Melinda Gainsford Taylor, Debbie Flintoff-King and Cathy Freeman, while others I read about in books.

One woman I wish I had met in my lifetime was Catherine Hamlin. When people now start to judge my overimaginative mind or query my age when it comes to my career in medicine, I draw on her story.

My final key that has helped me navigate the bumpy road of my life has been to seek out people who proved that all my crazy ideas and goals were possible.

Catherine graduated from medical school in the 1940s. She then became an obstetrician and gynaecologist when few women were doctors, let alone surgeons. She could have chosen to stay in Sydney and likely made a fortune in gynaecology, being one of the only females available. But she and her husband Reginald (also an obstetrician) wanted to make a difference in the world, so they headed off to Addis Ababa in Ethiopia on a short-term secondment. When she was there, she became aware of the thousands of Ethiopian women who were suffering horrific obstetric injuries due to lack of medical care and a long obstructed labour. Without access to medical assistance such as caesarean section, the baby often died inside the mother but still had to be birthed. This protracted labour left the women with obstetric fistulas (an abnormal opening between the bladder or bowel and the birth canal). These women, left urinally or faecally incontinent, are often outcasts from their villages, kept away from their children. Catherine decided to stay and pledged her life to this cause. Over her 60 years in Ethiopia, she set up six fistula hospitals, a midwifery school, and helped heal more than 60,000 women of their obstetric injuries. Incredible, isn't it? What I also find inspiring is the fact she was still practising as a doctor in her early nineties. Imagine how many times people would have doubted her or questioned her moving to Ethiopia with her young son and husband. She simply didn't listen and bravely took on the challenges. Sadly she passed away in 2020, but she leaves a legacy larger than most.

Catherine wrote a great book called *The Hospital by the River* (Pan Macmillan, 2001) which I encourage you to read. In a nutshell, if I can be half the woman she is, I will rest happily in my grave. So, when I am struggling for motivation, or someone questions my ability, I think *What would Catherine do?*

She'd push on. She would defy the odds and find a way. Life is about having faith in your journey and finding people who prove the impossible is possible.

My greatest challenge

So that's it folks: my life in a nutshell. Of course, there are many other chapters that helped shape who I am today; however, the ones I chose to share with you are the ones that I feel gave me my backbone, built my resilience and put fire in my belly.

We all define success differently, but I have learned that success is not just about winning races or having the perfect career. It is about finding that inner fulfilment and belief that you are fabulous just the way you are. I have met some amazing people in my life and I have learned that those who accept their imperfections and openly share their flaws often walk the tallest.

Don't get me wrong: you can't be tough all the time. No matter how much self-belief you have acquired or how hard you apply yourself, life is a roller-coaster and at times we are all derailed. We just must hope there are more ups than downs and use the unexpected turns to re-evaluate our plans.

I found a resilience through the village of people who surrounded me. I have an unconventional life and an even more eclectic family, but I wouldn't change it for the world.

My life competing for Australia was extraordinary; my new career in medicine fills my heart with purpose; and my children complete me. The tough times taught me more than they hurt me, and I found a resilience through the village of people who surrounded me. I have an unconventional life and an even more eclectic family, but I wouldn't change it for the world.

My greatest challenge these days is the mother guilt that rages and rips through my heart as I try to fit in all my competing commitments. But I hush that voice and think of Catherine Hamlin. My goal is to try to leave the world a better place.

I hope you learn from my mistakes, laugh at my quirkiness and remember that people will always have varying opinions and make judgements. Ultimately, it's up to you how much weight you give their ideas and intentions. Use them as fuel for a goal or ignore them: be the author of your own life.

> Looking into the mirror, she realised she wasn't shattered; she was the perfect reflection of the journeys she'd been on.
>
> **Jana Pittman**

Thank you

My life has been touched by so many wonderful people who have helped shape me into who I am: my coaches, my mentors and my friends. Thank you for being my backbone when things got rough.

To everyone who contributed your wisdom to this book, you are amazing.

To my loving and inspiring parents, thank you for always having my back and teaching me the benefits of hard work.

To my kids, I love you deeply; you are my everything. x